A Brilliant Night is not a "how-to book[...] traditional biography of one family's e[...] this book offers us, its readers, so mu[...] this glimpse into a personal journal–[...] hope and encouragement to all of u[...] otherwise.

In her stories, Juli Able does not shy away from the difficulties of the adoption journey, yes, even a Christ-led, obediently-responded-to one. In these challenges, though, Juli clearly reveals that God will be with us on our journeys every step of the way.

This book flows from the author's deep and rich life with God. As you read it—and I cannot recommend highly enough that you do—I would suggest that you consider reading just a chapter a day. As you do so, I believe you, like me, will find yourself pondering each message with God throughout your day. In the end the true gift of this book is that it gives its readers the gentle, welcoming invitation to look for and be sensitive to the movement of God in our lives.

—**Dr. Timothy J. Harben,** Spiritual Director and
Adjunct Faculty, North Park Theological Seminary

Juli Able is a masterful storyteller. I know of very few writers today who write with such brilliance and color, whose real-life stories draw us into an inward journey of discovery. *A Brilliant Night* is deeply invitational and transformational. As I read this book, I discovered a gentler way of being with myself and a life with God that drew me beside the still waters rather than drove me to exhaustion. Through Juli's adoption story I met a God who longs to be alongside us, offering comfort through the hard, unfathomable places of pain and unknowing. This is a book I will put on my bedside table, as a companion to remind me of whose I am and who I am.

—**Brenda Golden**
Founder and Director of The Agape Center for Spiritual Formation
Co-founder of Land of a Thousand Hills Coffee Company
Co-founder of St. Peter's Place Anglican Church

This book is just like its author—a gentle companion. Every page brims over with love, honesty, and humility. Juli *notices*—from seaweed to basketball games—and helps open our eyes to appreciate God's presence in our own world. She asks the kinds of questions that accompany a journey, an adventure. I share Juli's journey through the hard, unexpected, and unfinished within the context of adoption, but her example and insights will bring comfort and courage, perhaps even some guidance to the very unique path where you find yourself. Juli invites us to see and trust that *yes*, our destination is worth everything—freedom in Christ!

—**Nancy Griffith,** Renovare Institute graduate,
adoptive mom, and friend of Jesus

One of the reasons I love to spend time with my friend Juli is her ability to see and breathe in God's wisdom in whatever her circumstances. Her superpower of being profound and simple at the same time are on full display in this collection of stories, as is her ability to strip away the extra, leaving just enough for one to find God and His love.

This book is full of relatable stories that can encourage us all to slow down, listen more closely, and lean into what God wants to reveal to us in our everyday moments. Through her simple and authentic insights, Juli demonstrates that our struggles and sacrificial love are not always tied up in pretty packages. And that does not negate His presence right smack in the middle of them.

—**Jenny Bramel,** M.S.W.,
Director of Parent Ministry, encourager of humans

Juli's story is a breath of fresh air in a world where everyone else seems to have it together. Her vulnerability about the struggles of following God in times where it feels as if you can't see or feel Him is a reminder to all of us to seek to trust God more than seeking to please Him.

—**Alan White,** Family Life Pastor, Mount Pisgah United Methodist Church

In *A Brilliant Night* Juli Able writes a beautiful story of hope in hard circumstances. Although it can be hard to accept, I believe Juli is correct when she says that a deeper life with God lies beyond our failures and successes. In many cases, a deeper life with God lies beneath whatever had done the most to break us.

This resonated with me deeply. Juli doesn't shy away from sharing how a season of darkness and unraveling in her family affected her spiritual journey with God. There's messiness, anger, fear, and rejection. But through it all, there's also God. He's in the muck, in the pierced and broken hearts, in the unresolved conflicts and things left unsaid. As Juli navigates through the pain of failing relationships, she also finds surprising places where God shows up—walks along beaches, heart-shaped sunglasses, and evergreen trees.

I would recommend *A Brilliant Night* to anyone going through a hard time, where hope has waned and God seems distant. I think when we can come to the place where we love and accept God's will beyond the outcome we desire, then we might have arrived in our hearts where He intended to meet us all along.

—**Graham Garrison,** magazine editor and
author of *Hero's Tribute* and *Legacy Road*

A Brilliant Night

Experiencing God in the
Hard, Unexpected, and Unfinished

JULi ABLE

ELECTRIC
MOON
PUBLISHING

Published by Electric Moon Publishing, LLC

©2022 A Brilliant Night: Experiencing God in the Hard, Unexpected, and Unfinished / Juli Able

Paperback ISBN: 978-1-943027-57-6
E-book ISBN: 978-1-943027-58-3

RELIGION / Christian Living / Inspirational
RELIGION / Christian Living / Personal Growth

Electric Moon Publishing, LLC
P.O. Box 466
Stromsburg, NE 68666
info@emoonpublishing.com

Library of Congress Cataloging-in-Publication data available. LLCN: 2022912877

Cover Design and Interior Design by Lyn Rayn / Electric Moon Publishing Creative Services

Printed in the United States of America

ELECTRIC MOON PUBLISHING
www.emoonpublishing.com

The stories in this book are true,
with some details adjusted to respect
the privacy of those involved.

Contents

Prologue

*T*he stories in this book about my family's challenges are vague. This is intentional to protect the privacy of others and to allow these stories a broader reach. While I choose not to delve into our specifics, the following background information may help.

During our application process for adoption, we learned about reactive attachment disorder (RAD). The disorder was briefly mentioned in a required online slide show as a rare condition that could devastate adoptive families. Two slides in a twenty-minute presentation touched on this and shared only the most overt symptoms to watch for. To be honest, I felt immune—as though it couldn't happen to us. Maybe because it was presented as uncommon; maybe I ignored it because I deeply wanted to adopt; and also at play may have been an erroneous belief that our investment in careful discernment and prayer eliminated this already-remote risk. It was easy to ignore, until it wasn't.

Experts explain that "RAD develops when a child's brain is impacted by trauma, often abuse and neglect, during the first few years of life."[1] Children affected with RAD have difficulty forming emotional attachments to others and difficulty seeking or accepting physical or emotional closeness. They may be unpredictable, hard to console, and hard to discipline.[2] This condition is more common than often presented, as a 2004 study illuminates: "While RAD is rare in the general population, it is common in abuse cases. In one study of toddlers in foster care who had been maltreated, 38-40% of the children met the diagnostic criteria for RAD. Many older children who have delayed disclosure of their early abuse also suffer from undiagnosed RAD."[3]

Often the primary target of a child's RAD behavior is the adoptive mom. "She is the person to whom (the adoptive child) most wants to connect and the person with whom it seems the most dangerous. A mother can't be trusted. She may be an abandoner."[4] Because of this, "the child with RAD goes to great lengths to push away Mom, often via triangulation and manipulation. Many moms say they 'feel crazy' because no one else sees or experiences the same RAD behaviors as she does."[5] At the same time, "the child with RAD often charms (other caregivers and significant adults) and leads them to believe that Mom is unreasonable."[6] This dynamic often creates confusion as to the nature of the conflict between the child and Mom because other caregivers are not directly affected by it. This confusion can result in a lack of understanding and support.[7]

In clinical research, participant caregivers, particularly adoptive mothers, described feelings of exhaustion, fragility, shock, surprise, a sense of unrelenting burden, and unpreparedness for the intensity of challenging behaviors of children with RAD.[8] Feelings of failure, disappointment, and confusion related to the unpredictability of their children with RAD's inappropriate attachments to others were shared throughout. Caregivers of children with RAD expressed intense worry, anxiety, and stress surrounding parenting and caregiving their children.[9]

RAD looks different across individuals. I initially experienced it as a void in our adopted son, James, and his avoidance of me. As long as I kept my distance, things appeared to be okay on the surface. But if I sought connection and attachment, or worse, if I sought to parent with boundaries and instruction, symptoms escalated. Even with significant professional therapy, our daily home life was a minefield of dissociation, manipulation, hostility, lack of trust and controlling behaviors, provoking anger in others, superficially and selectively charming others, chronic lying, and creating conflict and distrust among and between others (splitting or triangulating relationships).

These behaviors were symptoms of complex trauma—which was incredibly heartbreaking—

stemming from wounds and sustained childhood trauma beyond what we could imagine. Placed in a similar circumstance, anyone would likely display symptoms or no longer be alive. I believe they enabled James to survive his first ten years of life. And I share them here to illuminate our reality.

Through the years of navigating this, I've observed human nature, in seeking to understand, also wants to assign fault to someone. Perhaps this is innate in our attempts at making sense of something. Yet in blaming, we miss a grander invitation. Amor Towles in his book *A Gentleman in Moscow* describes such an opportunity when struggle crosses our path. If we refuse blame, shame, and self-pity, we discover an invitation into a community he names "The Confederacy of the Humbled." Here's what he says:

> "The Confederacy of the Humbled is a close-knit brotherhood whose members travel with no outward markings, but who know each other at a glance. For having fallen suddenly from grace, those in the Confederacy share a certain perspective. Knowing beauty, influence, fame, and privilege to be borrowed rather than bestowed, they are not easily impressed. They are not quick to envy or take offense. They certainly do not scour the papers in search of their own names. They remain committed to living amongst their peers, but they greet adulation with caution,

ambition with sympathy, and condescension with an inward smile."[10]

This is where I desire to be—on a journey with friends. My hope is that you will accept this open invitation to discover the divine and a community of friends in your hard, unexpected, and unfinished places. Join me?

Introduction

I've been thinking lately about Abraham and his experiences with God, especially that time in the thick of night under a canopy of stars. The Bible tells us that God brought him outside and spoke, saying "Look toward heaven and count the stars, if you are able to count them. . . . So shall your descendants be" (Genesis 15:5 NRSV).

Maybe Abraham had been sitting in his tent, discouraged and lost in thought, when all of a sudden, he heard a booming, unmistakable voice tell him to go outside. And that same distinct, audible voice told him to look up and spoke of promised descendants more numerous than the stars shining overhead.

Or maybe it was more like this: One evening as the hustle and noise of a workday wound down and things fell quiet, familiar voices of doubt, fear, and discouragement began to clamor within Abraham. They pummeled him with questions, problems, and a litany of what-ifs. Abraham took in his temporary tent accommodations, his ever-aging, still-barren wife, Sarah, and the lonely quiet of a home with no children. He had listened and followed God as best he knew how. He had been promised a new homeland and a really big family, yet nothing was happening. He fled outside, needing a change of scenery and some fresh air. In the growing darkness he sat in the quiet and sought God. As the sky deepened from purple to navy to black, he released those swirling questions and nagging doubts to God— simply saying them out loud and sending them off with the wind.

As his insides calmed, he began to notice the stars. One by one they emerged, slowly filling the sky until they crammed every corner and every empty space. It became difficult to distinguish one from another. He had never seen so many stars. Stunning and magnificent!

He sat, mesmerized by the sparkles of light animating the dark. Quietly it dawned on him. *God desires to give me descendants like these stars . . . glorious and too many to count*. A deep peace washed over him, and he simply knew: this was God's presence *with* him and God's promise *for* him. The picture of that star-filled sky stayed with Abraham, drawn in his mind's eye so that when doubting voices tried to invade again, Abraham simply recalled the stars and clung to the promise God had given him.

My own experiences with God have been more like this latter version: subtle and slow, asking me to show up and make room to get quiet, to deliberately ask my questions and to speak my doubts into a dark night that is anything but empty.

Maybe people thought Abraham was crazy when he tried to describe what happened that night. It's hard to put into words how you know when a starry night sky is a meeting place with God.

This collection of stories shares the sparks of light that began to fill my own dark season. My son once captured its essence with a question: "Why did God ask us to adopt and then let it fail?" That question frames my story. It's an important question because the one who is asking matters, as does our adoption and our adopted son, James. It also gets to the heart of a deeper question: can I trust God?

But this is not an adoption story. I do not presume to speak with authority on adoption. Nor can I answer my son's question. There are and always will be secret things that belong only to God. He is Mystery. But what I can do is share what He has revealed about Himself, me, and His love, character, and faithfulness. These revelations are mine.

And yet these experiences are not just for me. There is a journey here, one that is open to all of us. A deeper life with God lies beyond our apparent failures and even our successes. It lies beneath whatever experience or circumstance has done the most to break us. In fact, that can be the doorway.

At least, that is where I discovered *my* doorway.

Perhaps you may find hints of yours here as well.

> *In the year that my dream died, I saw the Lord as never before. Then I said, "This is all my fault. I'm not enough, and I can't make this better." And He saw and forgave and provided—again and again and again.* (my adaptation of Isaiah 6:1–7)

And this is my account of His faithfulness . . .

Campfire Conversations

A family friend quietly slipped away from our campfire circle, excusing himself to "search for firewood." Then, precisely at the cliffhanger of my dad's ghost story, he jumped into our midst with an "AHHHH!" disguised as our favorite ghost, Granny White. Our screams could be heard five miles away. But apart from Granny White and a few other instances, time around the fire has been peaceful, relaxing, full of laughter and stories, and also quiet spaces. Childhood camping trips and the campfires especially are some of my fondest memories. There is something mesmerizing about a fire. It lends itself to deep, thoughtful conversations, with permission for shared silence and for words to come slowly.

As you get to the end of each story in this book, you'll find questions intended for a space like that.

The questions are reflective in nature—possible conversation-starters with God for your own journey. They come with a word of caution: don't rush the conversation. Allow for silence to let things settle. Don't try to answer the questions based on what you already know about God. Sometimes you have to sit long with a question or wait a while for God to respond. And a word of encouragement: God *wants* connection with you. Let Him be an equal conversation partner. It's not all on you. Make space to listen as well as to talk to Him. Having another person to listen and process with can be helpful too.

Campfire Conversation
Introduction

1. Do you desire a deeper (more connected and mutual) life with God? Why or why not? What do you desire? Have you/can you share this with Him?

2. Where have you experienced discouragement, disappointment, or apparent failure? Are there areas in your life where it seems nothing is happening? What voices and feelings surface in these areas?

3. What helps to calm your insides? Maybe being in nature, tuning into your breathing, engaging with your five senses, sitting in a quiet church (these are just a few practices others have found helpful). What might it look like for you to spend some time letting things settle? And then ask God your questions and share your feelings with Him. Do that and let it be enough for now. Resist the urge to try to answer your questions with your own reason or your own understanding of God.

Patience

*T*he ground shook as we rounded a corner on a packed dirt road in Kampala's outskirts. As the orphanage and school came into view, it was quickly obscured by hundreds (literally) of children running toward us, singing, "Wel-a-come!" This was our first trip to Uganda to meet James, our future adopted son.

Upon exiting the van, children of all ages pressed in, touched us, gifted us with their smiles and excitement, and embraced us in their love and welcome. I'd never experienced welcome as I did in Uganda.

As we made our way toward a campus building, somehow a tiny hand found its way into mine. Miraculous that in the mass of people the little girl it belonged to could get that close and hold on! Yet once my friend Patience found me, she stuck like glue. Every visit we made to the campus that week, she was there. She brought a quiet insistence and determination to her self-assigned task of staying by my side. She had a fierce scowl that kept others from usurping her spot. I enjoyed her quiet company and even began to anticipate it. I never had to go looking for her. She found me.

At some point during the week, I wondered about my new companion. Her name felt like a beacon—a light of sorts, to guide and accompany me on this new journey. She began to feel essential. I missed her when she was in class (although once she snuck out of class to find me).

I learned about patience, the virtue, through Patience the person. Patience, I discovered, is more than a courteous manner or a pasted-on smile that puts up with people. Patience has more substance than that. Patience is "an ability to face trouble without blowing up or hitting out. Its opposite is resentment toward God and others, and its counterfeits are cynicism or lack of care," as Timothy Keller teaches.[11]

Patience shows up, adapts, and stays with—perhaps silently and in the background, like my new friend. She doesn't draw attention to herself, but she sits in your lap and keeps other intruders, like resentment and discouragement, at bay. Quiet as she is, she's not afraid to kick them out of your lap, where she belongs. She can be a bit stubborn and immovable at times. Thank goodness, because I didn't realize how very much I would need her!

And here's the thing: I just showed up, and patience was there. I didn't earn her, achieve her, create her. She was and is a gift—a quiet insistence, a deep breath, a squeeze of my hand, reminding me that I'm not alone and I can be present with things as they are right now. I can wait, and I can trust. My only work was simply to listen to patience, give her space, let her lead. I'm not saying that I never sat with, ate with, or slept with resentment. But somehow patience always found her way back to me. God gave me patience as a companion for the journey.

Patience, I've learned, quietly endures.

She keeps you company while you wait.

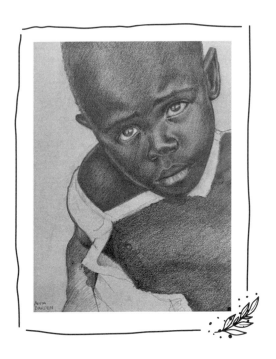

This is a sketched drawing of the real, one-and-only Patience. It captures her expressive face. Her eyes say something to me—and though I'm still trying to figure out exactly what that is, it lingers with me, imploring me not to leave, not to give up. Maybe what she's saying is "Stay."

Campfire Conversation
Patience

1. Where have you experienced welcome? What about it was special and/or helpful for you? Do you think God was present somehow in that experience? If so, how?

2. Where have you encountered patience? How would you describe it? What might be the difference between *willingly* and *willfully* engaging patience?

3. How might God be inviting you to stay with Him in a difficult or unresolved place? (This doesn't mean staying in an unhealthy, harmful environment. Sometimes this may look like staying with God while moving/letting go/releasing external realities.)

4. As you look around in your present moment, is a companion nearby or one you might desire (perhaps a virtue such as patience, humility, hope, peace, faithfulness, self-control, goodness, love, truthfulness, or joy)? If one of these stands out to you (either by way of attraction or resistance), give it some attention. Get to know this companion.[12] If you're unsure where to begin, the best starting place of all is simply to ask God for a companion and then pay attention. As you engage, beware of the temptation to implement

and practice the virtues of God without God. (This seems obvious, but it's a strong temptation.) Always engage *with* Him. He has the needed kindness and energy available to support your journey.

Joy

*A*n internal alarm incessantly blared; an uneasiness settled in. I could not shake it. And it grew increasingly difficult to ignore and pretend. Adoptive mothers often have a sixth sense about attachment issues early on. This was true for me when it came to our new son. During our second trip to Uganda, we'd begun to spend significant time with James when we were granted guardianship, but were awaiting permission for him to travel home to the United States with us. As I cautiously stepped into mothering him, something seemed terribly wrong, but words failed. At the time, I only had a sense of all the lights turning off inside. I felt dark and cold. Perhaps it was my close proximity to someone who felt dark and cold himself on the inside. This vacancy (or lack of attachment) was not familiar.

It scared me. I desperately wanted to go home to my biological sons, who could attach and were attached, who could reciprocate a sense of connection and love. It wasn't that they needed me so much; I needed them and longed for the sense of grounding and belonging in our home.

It took years to admit and accept that it was okay for me to have feelings like that. But needing to feel safe and secure is simply human. And it's okay to need it. It's okay to be human. *Everyone* has permission in challenging circumstances to be human—to need what we need and feel what we feel. And what I felt in that moment was an unraveling and shrinking, even as more was being asked.

Three weeks into our trip, we set out for yet another day during a string of seemingly endless days we'd spent waiting for whatever we needed to travel home with James. I pulled my husband aside as we left the hotel and whispered, "I'm tired of being stretched beyond what I can stretch." And then we were off. I was scheduled to teach a lesson to teen girls. And I had nothing.

The words of a song by Lindsay McCaul kept playing through my head.[13] They described encountering a sudden storm while attempting to follow God. They articulated my feelings and desires. I had started out confident and unwavering but now felt afraid. I didn't want to leave. I just wanted God to take my hand and reassure me: "You didn't get this wrong. You aren't alone."

Yet, very much alone in the back of the van, I held out my hand and silently prayed. *Take my hand. Take my hand. Take my hand.*

Nothing happened.

We arrived at the orphanage to the sound of seven hundred and something happy, excited children. And what do you know? A companion found me again! As had happened in my previous trip to Uganda, a little girl made her way through the throng of children, stayed very close, and made it clear that the space next to me was occupied. This time, her name was Joy. She was a precious little one with a shy smile and tinkling laughter that found its way into her eyes. Her name fit her well. I was glad for the company, and we set off together to share the lesson I was ill-prepared to give.

Then I heard good news. The children had just completed a *day* full of lessons and were ready to play outside. That, I could do! All the while, Joy stayed close, asking for the ball again and again until she tired of the ball, tugged on my skirt, and asked for a baby doll instead. Sweet Joy! As I played with these children, I lost myself and the clinging darkness.

It wasn't until we returned to our hotel that evening and I reflected on the day that I realized: from the moment I stepped out of the van, Joy had grabbed hold of my hand and never let go. Surprise and delight swept over me. God heard my prayer! God took my hand! And He didn't just take my hand; He placed JOY in my hand. "Joy," says Dallas Willard, is "a pervasive *sense*—not just a thought—of well-being: of overall and ultimate well-being . . . for joy, *all* is well, even in the midst of specific suffering and loss."[14]

God chose this unexpected gift for me. At the beginning of a journey through a dark, painful valley, He set joy before me. It made me think of Jesus, who endured pain and disregarded shame by focusing on the joy set before Him (Hebrews 12:2 paraphrase).

I love that joy, like patience, isn't superficial and forced, but resides somewhere deeper. I love that it's not always loud and jumping up and down; it can be quiet. I love that it's not dependent upon cheery, easy circumstances; it's more resilient than that. And I love that I don't have to muster it up; it's something God places in my outstretched hand.

Joy and I during one of our many visits to the orphanage and school. She was a surprising and sweet companion on some long days.

Campfire Conversation
Joy

1. Does joy feel like a misfit in your tough situations? Why or why not? How does Dallas Willard's definition and/or Jesus's example help to make room for joy?

2. What do you love about joy?

3. Do you sense that you have permission to be human (to feel what you feel and need what you need) in your places of struggle? Why or why not? What do you need? What do you feel? Have you/can you share that with God?

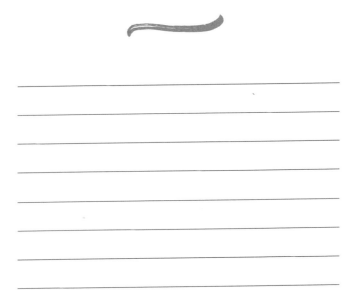

_____

_____

_____

_____

_____

_____

_____

Seaweed

*T*he world's most beautiful beaches can sometimes be anything but.

And the culprit is seaweed.

Seaweed can turn a beach of wispy-soft, fine white sand beside clear emerald water into a stinking, rotten, bug-infested swamp. I spend a week at a favorite beach every year. Last year during most of that visit the seaweed was so thick and rotten that people turned away from the beach altogether. At the time, I wanted to order a bulldozer to carry it all away, thinking nothing short of that would do the trick. But to my surprise and delight, a storm in the night whisked all the seaweed out to sea, out of sight and (thankfully) smell.

So this year when I returned, I began my walk down the quiet, state-park beachfront with trepidation, fearing the seaweed would repel me again. Things began kind of iffy. A fairly wide string of seaweed stretched before me. It was annoyingly positioned right at the sweet spot for beach walking.

I had to pay more attention to the seaweed than I wanted to, and that frustrated me. Instead of losing myself in the waves' rhythm, the sea's beauty, or the endless sky, I needed to attend to the mess at my feet.

Trudging along, my mind turned to the unpleasant, stinky things in my life—"seaweed things" I wished God would magically wash away, but He hadn't. They were frustrating and troublesome on the surface. As I looked more deeply, they were hurtful, maybe harmful, certainly fear-inducing, and seemingly beyond my ability to understand, much less control. I was in a mess. *We* were, actually. A big mess. And this was supposed to be the "honeymoon period" of adoption when things usually went well.

I began to talk to God about these hurts and fears, wondering if He was listening, questioning if He was aware . . . and mostly doubting He would intervene.

At several points along my walk I considered turning back. The seaweed string seemed to stretch on forever.

Yet something inside nudged me to keep going. Just keep moving forward. *Just be where you are. You can't fix this. You can't change this. Keep walking.*

So I did. And as I continued, I encountered a surprise: a seaweed heart. And a little farther down the beach, a seaweed-inscribed "I love you." They made me smile. Then they made me think. My thoughts traveled beyond imagining a teenager's romantic plot to this: *I am looking at a message of love written with the very stinky, frustrating substance I want distance from.*

A question surfaced: What if this scenario that presently looks like and feels like rejection is actually a message of love somehow, somewhere farther down the path? What if God is using the very trials in our way to tell us He loves us?

An acute sense told me that I wasn't as alone as I thought or felt. Here I had a reminder of sorts, written with yuck, that I am loved. I am seen. I am not alone. He can transform this mess into something good.

What if I were to lean into this stink instead of turning my nose up at it? What if confidence was a companion—that I'm precisely where I am supposed to be instead of the self-doubt I felt because the muck appeared permanent and endless? What if He was interrupting this mess with a message of love? What if by refusing to stay present with God, I had missed that message?

Lord, I don't want to miss anything from You. And I'm cool with this. You can tell me I'm loved by using yuck. It doesn't change or alter the message. In fact, maybe it strengthens the message. I don't need to fear the yuck because You can make it into something different . . . something beautiful.

The messages of love I found as I just kept walking the beach.

1. Where are you finding "a mess right at your feet"? What thoughts go through your head about it? What feelings do the mess cause to surface in you?

2. What would it look like for you to slow down and stay with these "seaweed things," as opposed to avoiding them or trying to clean them up? How might you look for God right there in the midst of the mess?

3. What do you (honestly) want to say to God about the hurts and fears lying under the mess? What do you want Him to do? Have you/can you share that with Him?

4. In what ways are you doubting yourself because of the yuck? What would confidence in yourself and in God look like?

5. In reflecting back, can you see instances when God interrupted a mess to tell you that you are loved?

4

Music

My memory is horrible. Information goes in but it seems to evaporate. Often I couldn't tell you in the evening what I read that morning. Give me a set of instructions, a program, a chart or graph, and my eyes gloss over.

But give me a song, and that's different. Lyrics are warehoused on my permanent memory drive. I trace this back forty years to my best friend and me belting out Eddie Rabbitt from the rear of my family's station wagon, at the top of our lungs, with hand motions. Songs tend to materialize and play in my head even while I sleep. I think God has a way of making His words like songs for me. He knows I need help remembering them. So He connects things worthy and valuable to things more tangible and plays them on repeat throughout my day.

Hosea 14 became such a song that God loved to sing over me.

A short four months into our adoption, I was in way over my head. One random November morning I stumbled upon this: "We will say no more, 'Our God,' to the work of our hands. In you the orphan finds mercy" (Hosea 14:3b NRSV). I noticed that the orphan finds mercy (undeserved forgiveness, a no-questions-asked new beginning) in God (not in Juli). And since I was fresh out of mercy, this promise met such a need.

I found permission to lack because mercy was *supposed* to come from God. The internal refrain, "I should be more forgiving, patient, loving, calm, flexible, compassionate, accepting," was not His voice. In the words of Hosea, my frantic fixing—searching for support, strategies, and all manner of experts—while not bad, wouldn't save us. The work of my hands (or anyone else's) would not rescue us.

So I could seek these sources of help *without the panic*. I could wait, breathe, sleep. This wasn't on my shoulders to figure out. I was not expected to save the day. Saving is God's job, not mine. "Savior" is a job description I cannot nor should I ever try to fill.

Reading further, I saw that more promises appeared in this obscure chapter of Hosea. *God will heal his disloyalty. God will love him freely. He will take root and blossom and grow and be fragrant and add beauty.*[15] Pronouns in the chapter then shift from singular to plural. *They will live again under His shadow; they will flourish and blossom and be fragrant.*[16] I *so* loved that, because this adoption process had deeply affected everyone in my family. God saw *us* in this story too. He would tend to each of our needs.

And then a critical reminder: it is God who answers and looks after us. All good gifts come from Him. He is faithful, like an evergreen tree. Among the oak and maple and beech, evergreens can blend in. But when seasons turn and colder winds blow, while others lose their leaves, the evergreen remains the same.

I wrote down these words and spoke to God about them in the quiet of my heart. And time passed. As the strife and hurt continued in my home, I lost sight of these promises, and my hope dimmed. Three months later, I read, "The LORD came to help Sarah and did for her what he had promised" (Genesis 21:1 GW). This was Sarah, Abraham's ever-aging, still-barren wife, who waited alongside him for the big family God promised. Her lengthy wait stretched far beyond my three months. Returning to Hosea, I remembered and asked God again to fulfill what we could not for ourselves.

Fifteen months passed. And the strife and hurt continued in my home. I lost sight of these promises. And my hope dimmed. Strangely enough, one late spring morning I read again, "The LORD visited Sarah as He had said, and the LORD did for Sarah as He had spoken" (Genesis 21:1b NKJV). It felt like a gentle whisper from God: "The promises I make, I keep. They are not empty words from an uncaring god. Read Hosea again and let it strengthen you. I am for your good and your children's. Trust Me."

And so I read Hosea 14 again. God brought this truth back to my heart, like a song that comes in sleep. Except this time I paused: "I am like an evergreen cypress; your faithfulness comes from me" (Hosea 14:8b NRSV). In my kitchen stood a small evergreen cypress that a sweet friend had given me as a Christmas gift months before. *It never occurred to me, God, that Sallye's gift was a reminder of Your promise! Renewed and reconfirmed. In living color, something to touch and water and smell—a promise kept green and alive, helping me remember . . . He who promised is faithful.*

I loved that little tree. I cherished the friend who gave it to me and the God who promised faithfulness through it.

Three more months passed. And the strife and hurt continued in my home. I lost sight of these promises. And my hope dimmed. My husband and I were gifted a weeklong retreat to Steamboat, Colorado, by wonderful, discerning friends who knew we needed time away. A strenuous hike deep into the Rocky Mountain wilderness was the highlight. The morning after, in a book by Mark Batterson, I read this about George Washington Carver:

"[He] routinely got up at 4:00 a.m., walked through the woods, and asked God to reveal the mysteries of nature. Job 12:7–8

> was one of the most-circled promises in
> his Bible. "But ask the animals, and they
> will teach you, or the birds in the sky and
> they will tell you; or speak to the earth, and
> it will teach you, or let the fish in the sea
> inform you."[17]

As I was surrounded by incredible mountain wilderness, it occurred to me to ask God for encouragement of something I needed and perhaps had forgotten. I even had a sense that He wanted to. And so I asked Him.

Almost immediately the wildflowers came to mind. They were *everywhere*—all kinds and colors, their heavenly fragrance carried by mountain breezes. We even came across a yellow snow lily at our highest elevation point. It was amazing to discover such beauty thriving in extremes, and entirely on their own, untouched by human hands. No one planted, watered, or pruned them. No one covered them when temperatures dropped. I thought of what God says about flowers.

> If God gives such attention to the appear-
> ance of wildflowers—most of which are
> never even seen—don't you think he'll
> attend to you, take pride in you, do his
> best for you? What I'm trying to do here is to
> get you to relax, to not be so preoccupied

with *getting*, so you can respond to God's *giving* . . . Don't get worked up about what may or may not happen tomorrow. God will help you deal with whatever hard things come up when the time comes. (Matthew 6:30–33a, 34b MSG)

This connected with my boys and the turmoil in our home. God wanted me to consider these flowers. Under His care, they don't just survive. They thrive in the hard, the harsh, the extreme conditions. It's *all* His provision. Since He cares for wildflowers on remote mountain peaks that few ever see, He certainly cares about my boys and their worried, angry, confused hearts. He will place them exactly where they will one day . . . in their season . . . thrive. It won't be without difficulty or frustration. Still, He will supply what is needed in every remote, seemingly unreachable place.

I received a measure of peace with this reminder. Yet, it wasn't until I got home and looked over my pictures that I recognized what was hidden in plain sight: a lily coming up through the hard, snow-covered ground—a lily about to bloom. And "he shall blossom like the lily" (Hosea 14:5b NRSV). Here again, God sang His promise over me.

Time passed. And the strife and hurt continued, even escalated, in my home. The song escaped me.

I wonder if Sarah forgot as often as I did. Maybe she faltered through those ten years. And like me, perhaps she doubted more days than she believed.

And yet the promises stood, not dependent upon me, given and fulfilled by a faithful God in His perfect time. The promises seem closer when He reminds me He is here amid the strife and the hurt. But in reality, He and His promises are always here, so I can be here too. I can wait. I can breathe. I can rest. Not because I am faithful, but because He is. Faithful even to keep singing the song to me. And by doing so, He lends me His faithfulness time and again.

The Christmas evergreen I received
from my sweet friend Sallye,
reminding me, even with its fragrance,
that God is ever faithful.

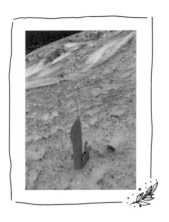

The hint of a new yellow snow lily popping up
on our Colorado trail.
At the highest elevation in the Mount Zirkel wilderness,
it blossoms . . . without my help.

These are ways God imprinted His promises on my heart, ways He sang His song over me—on repeat. Each refrain reshaped my heart to hold more room for His faithfulness.

> As I journey *through this life*,
> Your statutes are my song.
> (Psalm 119:54 VOICE)

"Assyria shall not save us;
    we will not ride upon horses;
we will say no more, 'Our God,'
        to the work of our hands.
In you the orphan finds mercy."
I will heal their disloyalty;
    I will love them freely,
    for my anger has turned from them.
I will be like the dew to Israel;
        he shall blossom like the lily,
        he shall strike root like the forests of Lebanon.
His shoots shall spread out;
        his beauty shall be like the olive tree,
        and his fragrance like that of Lebanon.
They shall again live beneath my shadow,
        they shall flourish as a garden;
they shall blossom like the vine,
        their fragrance shall be like the wine of
        Lebanon.
O Ephraim, what have I to do with idols?
        It is I who answer and look after you.
I am like an evergreen cypress;
        your faithfulness comes from me.
        (Hosea 14:3–8 NRSV, emphasis mine)

Campfire Conversation
Music

1. How do you feel about needing to have things repeated? What if God actually delights in reminding you? What does this say to you about God?

2. Have you ever asked God for a song in the night? (Maybe your "song in the night" is a special verse from Scripture, a phrase from a book, a written prayer or poem, or an actual song that reassures, comforts, steadies, or directs you. Ponder with God what your personal "song in the night" might be.)

3. What burdens seem to be on your shoulders to figure out and fix? How does that feel? What would it look like to trust God in this situation?

4. Have you ever experienced God in nature? What was that like? How was He revealing Himself to you in that? How might you go looking for God in creation? What have you been noticing lately in creation? What do you imagine God might desire to say to you about this?

5

Heart

"It is easier to find guides, someone to tell you what to do, than someone to be with you in a discerning, prayerful companionship as you work it out yourself."[18] This prayerful companionship Eugene Peterson describes is sometimes referred to as spiritual direction, and it's a means of caring for our souls through all of life.

Our family was encompassed by outside support—extended family, friends, an attachment therapist, a counselor, and a pastor. These extensions of God's care filled gaps all over the place—transportation, tutoring, childcare, tools and resources, wisdom, long walks, and prayer. But something was missing. Then I sought out a neighbor, someone I knew to be a spiritual director. I entered into this prayerful listening relationship not knowing much about it. In hindsight, I needed someone to help me find quietness so I could look for God. Though I desperately wanted *out* of the crisis, I really needed help finding God *in* it.

In one of our sessions as I articulated my struggle to connect with James, my spiritual director asked, "Have you ever asked God to show you James's heart?" She offered this freely, in reference to our adopted son, rather than forcing it. She didn't lead with "I think you should . . ." Yet I resisted. I wasn't consciously aware of my resistance at the time. I just *forgot* to do it, or ran out of time in my prayers, or thought about it briefly but never actually asked God for this. My spiritual director never asked again. She trusted God and me to work it out ourselves. Some things take time.

Nine months later I attended a large worship concert. At some point during the evening, that question just bubbled to the surface. Before I could think to resist it, I asked with eyes closed, "God, will you show me James's heart?" When I opened my eyes, the on-stage television screen was filled with the image of a heart. I can't remember the song that was playing, but I remember the image—a completely shattered heart with endless fragments and shards. No trace of whole-ness remained. Sketching it a few mornings later helped me ponder it with God. Though the heart was totally in pieces, it loosely held its shape. Large, yet invisible hands seemed to hold it together. Those had to be God's hands. Who else could cradle a shattered heart?

Sharing this experience in my next spiritual direction

session allowed the revelation to continue unfolding. I could see why any efforts to get close to James's heart were painful, both for myself in attempting to move toward him, and for James: the shards of his heart were razor sharp.

A couple of years later in a discouraged and self-doubting place, I revisited this prayer as I considered my son. James had strong survival instincts. Life had required that of him. He could adapt externally to new situations, but I questioned in my gut how much healing had really taken place. I didn't want to rely on my own understanding, so I sought God. I asked Him to show me James's heart again. Almost like retaking an X-ray, I wanted an outside source to assess any progress. Within a week, I experienced somewhat of an answer, though it wasn't exactly answering the question I had asked.

In the Bible is a story of Mary and Joseph escaping from King Herod to Egypt with their baby, Jesus. They eluded capture, but the threat that they fled from left a trail of dead baby boys in its wake. This was the legacy of King Herod's attempt to rid his world of future competition. The lines blurred between Mary and me as I imagined her feelings: shock (*I'm confused and disoriented by this sudden shift in circumstances*), guilt (*I should have warned these other mothers*), fear (*the opposition is overpowering*), amazement, gratitude, and relief (*oh, the incredible protection of God!*). Yet what rose above these feelings was a question. It screamed inside of me: *Why*? Honestly, it held accusation. *If You, God, are here to save, why aren't You? I thought You were coming to bring life, yet here is death because of You. For Mary, the death of so many babies. For me, the death of a dream, death of relationship. I don't understand. I didn't know that I signed on for this. I feel stuck, trapped, and afraid. And I am really angry.*

Intellectually I could answer my own questions, but that didn't change how I felt. So instead of disputing emotions with logic, which would only stuff messy feelings deeper, I opened up. I offered the mess and emotion to God. This was important because somehow this bleak disillusionment connected with my feelings around our adoption. I had found a screaming *Why?* within me.

Everyone in our family was hurting, including, and perhaps especially, James. He was miserable in our home, always confronted with the invitation and work and risk of intimate family relationship. Yet when I thought back to how I experienced him in Uganda, at his orphanage and school, surrounded by a makeshift family of sorts, he appeared to be happy. *Really* happy—relationally connected, and alive.

So I questioned everything we had done and what we were doing now. We'd uprooted him from his place of belonging for *this*? Was it our American arrogance that thought he would be better off here with us? There was no going back, but I wrestled with what moving forward was supposed to look like.

I wanted to help and heal, yet all I could see around me was more and multiplied hurt. In the quiet, this song from the Bible came to mind:

> But when I thought how to understand
> this, it seemed to me a wearisome task,
> until I went into the sanctuary of God . . .
> When my soul was embittered, when I
> was pricked in heart, I was brutish and
> ignorant; I was like a beast toward you.
> (Psalm 73:16–17a, 21–22 ESV)

As experienced by the poet, understanding felt out of reach. This sanctuary, a safe place with God, beckoned to me, a place to pause and listen. The word *embittered* in Hebrew means "grieved, sour, a bright red colour such as dazzles the eyes, bloodstained, affected with anger and pain."[19] The word *pricked* means "intensively to pierce, to assail anyone with sharp sayings, to be wounded, as if pierced through (with grief)."[20] These words drew a picture of Mary's heart. She desired to fill a life-giving role at God's invitation and to do that well. Yet the weight and pain of death as she arrived in Egypt bore down upon her.

Similarly, I wanted to be a mother, to care for and nurture a vulnerable life—a desire God planted in me. However, in my present circumstances I saw manipulation, deceit, and an unquenchable thirst for worldly and sometimes harmful things. Howard Thurman describes these as, "the hounds of hell that track the tail of the disinherited."[21]

God was showing me *my* heart this time, not

James's. It was embittered and pricked, bleeding a bright, dazzling red. It had been pierced over and over by the shards of a shattered heart. And I was acting like a "brute beast," harsh and insensitive—at times responding to James's survival mechanisms with frustration, despair, or rejection-in-kind. It seemed the hounds of hell that chase the disinherited also stalk those who are trying to get close to them, creating a vicious cycle.

Mary found sanctuary in Egypt, literally and figuratively. I soon discovered a place of refuge as well. During a walk in the woods at a nearby retreat center, I happened upon an image of a heart. Its description read, "the sacred heart of Christ," and it was dripping with blood. This gave me pause. I had beat myself up over my brute beast behavior, but this provided a perspective shift. In some small sense, perhaps this suffering was forming a heart more like Christ's. A resemblance was taking shape—my heart, while imperfect and in-process, was becoming more, not less, like His. I considered this image alongside the image of James's heart. Both hearts were wounded. One bleeds when pierced; the other shatters. What causes a heart to respond differently?

Maybe it depends upon the type of violence that has been done to a heart as well as the underlying condition of that heart. For a heart to shatter, it must be hard—like ice or glass. I wondered about the untold, likely unutterable circumstances that would cause a heart to harden and freeze over. Understanding deepened into compassion. Howard Thurman's writing illuminated a root of fear in James. Initially fear protects, but eventually it harms. Thurman wrote,

> Through bitter experience, (the disinherited) have learned how to exercise extreme care, how to behave so as to reduce the threat of immediate danger from their environment . . .[22] Fear becomes acute, in the form of panic or rage, only at the moment when what has been threat becomes actual violence. But the mere anticipation of such an encounter is overwhelming, simply because the odds are basically uneven. . . .[23] The result is the dodging of all encounters. The effect is nothing short of disaster in the organism.[24] This fear, which served originally as a safety device, a kind of protective mechanism for the weak, finally becomes death for the self. The power that saves turns executioner.[25]

Before we adopted James, he lived in constant anticipation of violence. He protected himself against the risk of care and nurture because in his experience it never lasted. The intimate love of a mom and dad presented the ultimate risk. And so he had become an expert dodger. But dodging love and connection leads to a hardness of heart and brings about another kind of death. Thurman's wisdom made me sad and afraid. Fear breeds deception, which becomes "a part of the nervous-reflex action of the organism."[26] Deception breeds hatred, until "a profound piece of surgery has to take place in the very psyche of the disinherited."[27]

Thurman continues, "How to do this is perhaps the greatest challenge,"[28] and he warns, "It ill behooves the man who is not forced to live in a ghetto to tell those who must how to transcend its limitations."[29]

A vague, far-away reality came into focus through this kind and wise teacher: only God could heal both of our broken hearts. Yet hope existed. God was the only surgeon for shattered and pierced hearts, and He saw ours clearly. "You have seen our affliction; you have known the distress of our souls" (Psalm 31:7b ESV, adapted).

In the meantime, my heart instinctively sought to respond to James's fear of intimacy, connection, and trust with my own fear of conflict, rage, and rejection. Sometimes I did respond in kind, but I was offered another way through these words of Thurman: "For the privileged and underprivileged alike, if the individual puts at the disposal of the Spirit the needful dedication and discipline, *he can live effectively in the chaos of the present* the high destiny of a son of God" (emphasis mine).[30]

In other words, "My flesh and my heart may fail, but God is the strength of my heart and my portion forever" (Psalm 73:26 ESV). Rather than finding a way out of the chaos, I was learning to be in it as my imperfect and in-process self with a God whose heart is whole and wholly love.

And this same God held both of our battle-weary hearts in His hands.

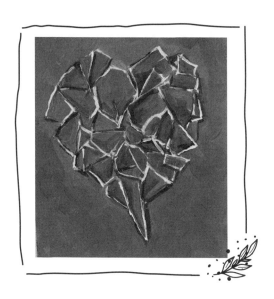

A sharply shattered heart

... and a bleeding, pierced heart.

Both are broken and in need of mending. When openly offered to God, He will do the slow work of healing.

Campfire Conversation
Heart

1. Are you are in the process of "working something out yourself" (as opposed to finding someone to tell you what to do)? Do you have any companions to share the messy process with? When was the last time you had such a conversation?

2. Is there a topic, question, or area of your life you've been avoiding with God? (or maybe avoiding God Himself?) How might you be unaware of your own resistance? Busyness, avoidance, boredom, rigidity, rationalizing, intellectualizing, and isolating are some indicators that you might be experiencing resistance, according to psychiatrist Gerald May[31], Jesuit spiritual director William A. Barry, S. J., and William J. Connolly [32] Do any of these hit close to home for you? What feelings surface? What might it look like to open this to God and perhaps someone else?

3. Have you ever considered asking God to show you someone's heart, maybe your own? What do you think the state of your heart is right now? Could you have blind spots regarding your heart? What might those be?

4. Do you think fear, deception, or hatred plagues your heart in any way? Have you/can you open that to God and/or another companion?

_____

_____

_____

_____

_____

_____

_____

_____

_____

_____

_____

_____

_____

_____

_____

6

Quilt

When my alarm sounded at 5 a.m., I cracked an eye and questioned my judgment. Only because five friends were gathering and learning to live life together with Jesus did I come round. That—and coffee. Good coffee helped.

One week as I left our gathering, a new friend from this group stopped me and placed a quilt in my hands. "I made this for you," she said. Continuing, she explained how she had visualized this quilt and felt prompted by God to make it before knowing who it was for. As she labored, cutting and stitching, a picture of me wrapped in the quilt formed in her mind's eye. There was a desire to comfort, to offer something that might feel like God wrapping me in His arms. She sensed meaning in the details: each different pattern of greens, blues, and golds represented one of my boys, including my husband, and their varied personalities, unique gifts, and interests. The dominant color and border were purple, and this symbolized God. I was represented by the little blue flowers scattered in the purple.

"When you lay the quilt out, you see the purple first," she said. "I believe when people interact with you, they see God first with a little of you thrown in the mix." I liked that. "Between you and God, your boys are surrounded," she added. "Even at the edges, He surrounds you all, and He holds it all together." She spoke to God as she quilted, asking Him to give us peace and wisdom in the midst of the chaos in our home. She asked Him to give us courage for the next step, that we might break out of fear-based, people-pleasing patterns and begin to see the present moment in the light of God's love. She hoped this quilt would always remind me that God has us.

From our conversation, I kept coming back to one thing: *He holds it all together*. This met me at my deepest fear. I was afraid of losing my family in this storm. And my friend's unexpected gift, inspired by God, saw that fear and touched my most vulnerable, shaken place.

A few mornings later, I spread the quilt, asking God to tell me more. In the silence, thoughts came to mind. They felt like whispers from God. And these whispers evoked a heart response in me. As I moved beyond logic and thought, a deeper knowing and connection with God began to take root.

Here is what I sensed as I made room for God and listened with my head and my heart.

- *You won't lose your boys. They are stitched into the fabric of your family—carefully, lovingly, thoughtfully, and expertly.* I felt safe.
- *You and they won't lose Me. I am in their midst and in your midst. All around. All encompassing. In between and within. I hold you all together. I hold each one together. I never let go. I stay. And I steady you.* I felt grounded.
- *You have a place here—then, now, and always. You haven't lost your purpose or worth to your boys or your family.* I felt valued.
- *I make you (all, collectively) one. I fit the pieces together. I know the ragged edges, the torn pieces, the places that don't seem to fit. I know how to work it all together for good.* I felt relief.

Some lyrics by Christy Nockels came to mind.[33] Her song was a prayer for mothers, and it fit beautifully with the whispers from God. As I listened to it—over and over and over—it felt as if I were wrapping myself in a quilt of God's love and care and protection. This was prayer too—giving God space to hold me in the promises. And in my smallness and weakness, I began to tangibly feel safe.

If Jesus were to ask me, as He asked so many, "What do you want Me to do for you?" I would have answered, "Jesus, I want You to hold my family together in this storm." God saw fear lurking deep in my heart, and He made this promise into material that I could touch: "In him all things hold together" (Colossians 1:17b NRSV).

A few weeks later, James's barely contained anger and rage exploded in my home. It left a gaping black hole in the wall, literally. But much worse were the words of hate that poured out of his mouth, screamed out, still echoing in my ears and in my heart. Every time I saw that hole, I heard those words again. I hated the hate in my home. I could not stand to look at that hole. I asked God, "How do I cover that black hole? Please give me something to cover the hole of hate in my wall and in his heart. I don't want hate to breed hate. I need another way."

Somehow (I can't remember how) I discovered Proverbs 10:12: "Hatred stirs up conflict, but love covers over all wrongs" (NIV). I wrote it in black Sharpie on some extra-large paper and taped it over the hole until we could have it repaired. Each time I passed that paper, I was reminded to ask God for a fresh supply of love to cover the wrongs. I didn't understand exactly what I was asking until I read it in a modern translation "Hatred starts fights, but love pulls a quilt over the bickering" (MSG).

Oh! A quilt! Had I not just received this quilt, I still wouldn't have understood. But ahead of my need, God provided. He reassured my deepest fears and told me that love wins; love is stronger; love holds it and us all together when rage and hate try to tear everything apart. Therefore fear, that hound of hell, can't get any closer because a soft and enduring quilt of love is wrapped around me. It's more resilient than hate that effortlessly kicked through two layers of drywall. Fear and hate don't win the day because His love already has. *I won't lose my family to this hate. I won't lose my boys to this hate. I won't lose my marriage to this hate. I won't lose myself or my sanity to this hate. And I don't have to fight it. I just get to live with love.*

God didn't remove the hate that day. Nor did He run from it or fight it. Instead, He showed me how to stay: wrapped in a quilt of love. This was why I woke up every week at 5 a.m. Not to learn more information about Jesus, not to follow some program or checklist that promised to make me more like Him or acceptable to Him. But to meet *with* Him. To grow in friendship with the One who stays, so that I could do likewise.

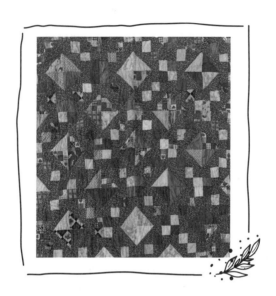

The beautiful quilt my friend Michelle stitched and prayed for me. It's not stored in a closet. We keep it in a basket by the sofa. It gets a lot of use in our family. For me it's an ongoing way to remember the feel of God's protecting love and to hear His whispered promise that again, today, He's holding us together.

1. Can you think of a time when you received an unexpected gift? What was it? How did it make you feel? Reflecting back, can you perceive any hint of God in that gift?

2. Imagine Jesus asking you what you are afraid of. Is that a hard question to answer? Maybe begin to pay attention to what you tend to avoid or what makes you angry or frustrated. He sees it more clearly than you do, so you could begin by asking Him.

3. What truth would be helpful for you to hear repeatedly? What do you keep forgetting? How can you creatively allow God to remind you (perhaps by wrapping up in a quilt, placing a note by your bed or a small symbol in your pocket, or maybe by listening to a song over and over again)?

7

Apple

Edgy. Uncooperative. And *antsy.* These are the words my friend used to describe a little girl she babysat. So my friend invited this little one outside and asked her to close her eyes and name every sound she heard . . . a bus, a leaf blower, birds, the wind blowing leaves, and so on. Then they noticed the smells. As the game continued, their insides slowed, their restlessness settled, and their stillness lingered. Later, the little girl asked, "Can we play that game again?"

I loved that story. The little girl sounded like me. There was an invitation in that, to be still and present. But it wasn't so easy. The contrary child in me was loud and bossy, naming all the other things I *should* do. Still, later that afternoon I pushed through and gave it a try. I went outside and sat down. I closed my eyes and listened and smelled and lingered in a quiet that was now more spacious. My mind turned to God with me on the porch. And instead of the bossy voice, I heard something gentler. This voice was curious. It wondered about my agitation and withdrawal. In my uncertainty I asked God, "Is there a reason for my funky mood? Where did I get off track?"

This came to mind: I thought I had been alone in my struggle, but I wasn't. I felt pushed, but no one had forced me.

And I knew right away where this fit.

Jeff and I had just returned from a four-day parents' retreat with James. *Retreat* seemed like the wrong name. Call it an *intensive*, maybe. But *retreat* implies rest and relaxation. This was hard, deep work, and instead of recovering afterward, I was unraveling. In this setting, children are expected to stay with their parents overnight at a summer camp type of facility. This was designed for connection and breakthrough.

But I *didn't* feel safe with James. I was afraid of his rage. And because his outside behavior didn't seem to match his insides, I felt uneasy.

So I reasoned with myself. *I should do this. All the other parents are. I shouldn't be afraid.* Such a bossy voice. I did ask God about it, wanting Him to tell me what to do. But I had only a general sense of freedom to choose. There was freedom, but I felt restricted. So I rationalized and listened to all the "shoulds" and forced it to happen.

Those nights were largely uneventful, except sleep eluded me. I was vigilant, stressed, and guarded. Even with my husband right there with his arm around me, I couldn't let go and sleep. Afterward, instead of being relieved, I felt numb, lifeless, and largely unavailable. It made no sense until that day on my porch. This was where I got off track: I had listened and followed the bossy and fearful voice.

Now I had space to listen for a quieter, gentler voice. I asked Jesus to speak into this, and I sensed Him say, *You are free to come in and go out, set boundaries, and speak up. You were covered at night in your husband's protection. You were safe. This experience of trauma can help you relate to what James feels and how fear is triggered.*

The quiet lingered, and I asked another question: "Jesus, what must You think of me? I'm so easily hooked by fear." Seemingly out of the blue, this thought surfaced: *You are the apple of My eye.*

Hmm, sweet. I thanked God for a measure of peace and assumed this conversation was over.

But the next morning, "apple of My eye" continued to echo. I found this connection in Deuteronomy 32:10 (VOICE): "The Eternal found Jacob out in the wilderness, out in an empty, windswept desert wasteland. He put His arms around him and took care of him; He protected him as the apple of His eye."

God putting His arms around me felt like protection and seemed to fit my circumstances that night. I became more curious.

Digging further, I discovered this: *the apple of the eye* is an ancient metaphor that literally means "the little man of the eye."[34] That's because when you stand very close and look deeply into someone's eyes, you can see your reflection in his or her pupils. If someone is the apple of your eye, you are focused intently on that person. This valuable and vulnerable part of the body where the reflection lies is provided layers of protection by way of eye sockets, eyelids, eyelashes, and eyebrows. Because it refers to what lies in the dark center of the eye, the American Revised Version of the Bible translates this same phrase as "in the middle of the night."[35] Symbolically, being the apple of someone's eye means you are deeply cherished and closely guarded by that person. "Whatever you treat as the apple of your eye is something about which you are massively protective."[36]

I didn't know God felt "massively protective" of me. Nor had I thought of myself as worth so many layers of protection. What I had assumed to be a nice, reassuring, albeit generic pat on the back was incredibly and uniquely fitting! I didn't realize God was "standing very close" in "the middle of the night." I suddenly felt safe, seen, and deeply loved.

It was far from a casual term of endearment, though I initially received it as such. This was special and fitting. This was real. God put His arm around me and took care of me. He protected me as the apple of His eye. When I let myself become still and draw close enough to look into God's eyes, I see the reflection of myself in the very center, something like I did on my porch that day. And when I'm antsy, uncooperative, and on edge, I need it most.

On those days may I become more willing to invite myself outside. May I be more available to play that game. May I increasingly recognize the gentle voice of my Father and distinguish it from bossier and more fearful voices. And may I trust more and more His protective love and lean in with my full weight.

My friend Andrea painted this apple. I love that it's still connected to the tree, receiving what it needs. An apple doesn't just grow on its own. It's always being fed. So if I am the apple of His eye, I receive not only God's protection but His provision as well.

> "How does an apple ripen? It just sits in the sun."
>
> —Thomas Merton, as quoted in
> James Finley's *Merton's Palace of Nowhere*[37]

 Campfire Conversation
Apple

1. What helps you to know when you're feeling antsy, uncooperative, or on edge? What does that look like or feel like in your body? What helps you to settle? What have you found that isn't helpful and tends to make it worse for you or negatively impact others?

2. Take some time to go outside and "play that game." Engage your senses one by one as you sit on your porch or perhaps while taking a *slow* walk. What did you notice? And what effect did it have on you?

3. How do you position yourself to hear from God? What helps you? What gets in the way? Have you ever mistaken God's voice for one that is bossy or fearful?

4. Have you ever considered yourself as the apple of God's eye? What does that mean for you? Where does it fit? How does it feel? Do you have doubts or questions? What do you want to say to God about this?

_____

_____

_____

_____

_____

_____

_____

_____

_____

_____

_____

_____

_____

_____

Shells

Sometimes I waffle. Ambivalence comes naturally to me. And one of the places it's bound to show up is at the uncertain precipice of success. I harbor mixed feelings about success. On one hand, success means goals are accomplished. People benefit. I feel productive and useful. Good results do good and feel good. On the other hand, I've seen organizations pursue success on behalf of God and seemingly leave God in the dust of that pursuit. It becomes more about them, their image, and endlessly achieving more. I've witnessed a godly leader's downfall via success. And I've been bogged down by numbers and budgets, spreadsheets and graphs that leave me questioning, "Where is God's heart here? What is His goal?" Drowning in numbers, I've also wondered: Would He do all this, would He spend everything for just one person?

In a season particularly numbers-focused, my frustration boiled over and I shared my honest heart with God. I was tired of chasing results, tired of sprinkling little bits into different lives who came and went. Investing deeply in one life appealed to me. This place of holy discontent led me toward a new invitation. A series of things, events, and people crossed my path, nudging me closer and closer to the new and, honestly, *surprising* idea of adoption. One of those things was a song by Aaron Crider titled "One Child Matters." The lyrics confirmed God's heart for every child. Another of those things was a large broken shell I found at the beach. My youngest son had brought me a similar shell a few days earlier. Holding both shells, I mulled over the meaning of this invitation.

We did not adopt because I heard a song and found a broken shell. That would be a foolish stretch. God slowly opened my heart to this idea in many ways and helped me see it was from Him. Discernment was a journey for both my husband and me, individually and together. Larry Warner, a pastor and spiritual director, counsels that where you sense God speaking, "follow slowly, as if you were seeking to determine whether or not a frozen lake was safe to walk on. Ask God to open you to promptings of the Spirit . . . whatever form they may take."[38] This took different forms at different times for my husband and me. Mine included songs and shells, scripture and wise counsel, fasting and waiting. Part of my waiting was for my husband as he discerned with God.

As can be the case, our steps were not always in sync, but we were both seeking God and held by God, wherever we were. The distance between us was not an indication that one of us was better or right while the other was wrong or less. In this instance, my husband's careful, deliberate, and slow-to-act posture afforded us confirmation, confidence, and a stronger unity for the difficult journey ahead. In our modern culture, slow can be mocked and derided as weak. But slow is often God's way.

And so our adoption journey unfolded slowly. During that time I occasionally wondered about the second broken shell. Why were there two? As someone eager to move ahead can be reluctant to share details that might slow things down, I hesitated to share this question with my husband. Then as our discernment culminated in the adoption of James, life became very challenging. I didn't want to share my question about two shells with *anyone*. One broken heart and life was turning our world upside down. Who could handle two?

The first year with James in our home was intense. I found myself at the beach after a year had passed, feeling adrift and terrified. Alone on a walk, I noticed a shell: large and whole. Of all that vast and sprawling seashore, this one whole shell riveted my attention. I pocketed it and begged God to make whole what was broken, knowing better than ever that only He could.

Another year passed of working for wholeness and talking with God about what it looked like. We were now in a season of intensive therapies for the traumatized and unattached. The gift I most wanted out of this place did not come. Nothing seemed to touch what needed healing inside of James. But we received other gifts, and one of the greatest was the other parents I met along the way. I tended to be quiet and reserved around them, as I usually am in newer environments, but one mom drew me out and welcomed me in. She was so vulnerable and out there and loving and broken. We stayed in touch, supporting and encouraging one another. For Christmas that year she gave me a gift book,[39] and her thoughtfulness touched me. I felt loved and cared for.

After the Christmas busyness subsided, I picked up that small book and read a story about a tired soul arriving at the beach just as dawn breaks. All that the beach offered awakened her senses and brought a measure of peace. The waves had recently deposited a new collection of shells and she began gathering some. Automatically, she bypassed a broken one in search of better, but then returned to the damaged shell. As she picked it up, she saw herself in its reflection and realized she was broken too.

Suddenly a light dawned in me. While reading this book I too, saw my reflection and realized: I was the second broken shell. There was no second broken child to bring into our family. Thank the good, good Lord! In my own way, I was broken too and needed healing. My relief wasn't any lack of love or something to feel guilty over. It simply reflected the fact that I had been operating beyond my (very human) limits. In the book, freshly aware of her brokenness, this tired, beach-walking friend responded to God. I had run out of words, so her prayers became my own. In them I discovered a deeper understanding of how life with God works and a deeper awareness of what He wants for us.

This broken friend was grateful that life hadn't completely crushed her. I echo gratitude that God is gentle with my weakness. She was grateful for the courage and strength to stay with what was broken. I echo relief that brokenness isn't something I'm expected to fix. My only task is to stay with God on this healing journey. She asked God for help to not compare her pain to others. I echo this acceptance: I'm not supposed to live life just like everyone else. She asked for strength to show her pain to others. I echo the affirmation: I want to freely be my own vulnerable self. She asked God to help her live more like a child, to linger and wonder. I echo with desire to mature into childlikeness, living slowly and present to the moment, able to see and receive the gifts it holds.

In all this, God sees and moves toward the broken, the ordinary, the small, the one. He longs to bring wholeness there. For Him, it's not about achieving success or eliminating failure. His goal for us is wholeness, and He desires to be whole with us. In fact, wholeness is a *with God* thing and a life-long work. While success might pretty-up the outside and push us toward results, wholeness seeks to envelop it all (including the brokenness) and be present in the moments as they slowly unfold.

Like Macrina Wiederkehr, an author and spiritual

guide, I was learning that speeding ahead in the fast lane of life, alternately trying to fix or run from challenges, impaired my ability to see well. "If you want to see the depths," Macrina wrote, "you will need to slow down. . . . Holiness comes wrapped in the ordinary. . . . Every tree is full of angels. Hidden beauty is waiting in every crumb. Life wants to lead you from crumbs to angels, but this can happen only if you are willing to unwrap the ordinary by staying with it long enough to harvest its treasure."[40] My ordinary shell on the beach that day was one such crumb leading to a treasure. In the end, I think God doesn't need our success. That's not the treasure. But He deeply yearns for us to come and be made whole.

> "There in solitude [Jesus] asked to be saved
> from the two imposters: success and failure."
> —G. B. Buttrick, *Prayer*[41]

I keep my broken shells on a shelf where I collect treasures that remind me of God's presence in the small, ordinary things. These remind me that God alone sees and repairs what is broken, including me.

Campfire Conversation
Shells

1. In what areas of your life do you desire to see success? How are you holding this desire—with open hands, closed fists, or something else? What might God desire in this area or situation or for this person? Have you/can you ask Him what His heart is here?

2. Is there an area of your life in which you are discerning direction? Have you noticed any promptings from God's Spirit? What does walking slowly with ears open toward God look like for you?

3. What could it look like for you to slow down and "unwrap the ordinary"? How do you practice slowness? Where have you discovered "holiness wrapped in the ordinary"? What did God want you to know in that?

4. Is there anything in your life that seems broken? Where do you desire wholeness? Which of the echoed statements in this story (summarized below) do you most need to hear? Picture yourself living into that with God. Describe what you see.

Summary Statements

- **Gratitude:** *God is gentle with my weakness.*
- **Relief:** *Brokenness isn't something I'm expected to fix.*
- **Acceptance:** *I'm not supposed to live life like everyone else.*
- **Affirmation:** *I'm free to be my own vulnerable self.*
- **Desire:** *God invites me (and I want) to be childlike; to live slowly and present to the moment, seeing the gifts it holds.*

9

Pearl

*T*he best ideas occur to me on my walks. Others tend to brace themselves when I return home and say, "So I've been thinking . . ."

Admittedly, while my walks can be the occasion of my best thinking, sometimes the opposite happens. On one occasion a battle ensued between the two possibilities—my mind was in turmoil, rehashing a conflict from the day before and second-guessing myself. I was "feeling off" but couldn't pinpoint the issue. Thankfully, at some point I returned to where my day began, which was in these words:

> God is *pure* light, undimmed by darkness of any kind. If we say we have an intimate

> connection with the Father but we con-
> tinue stumbling around in darkness,
> then we are lying because we do not live
> according to truth. If we walk *step by step*
> in the light, where the Father is, then we
> are ultimately connected to each other
> *through the sacrifice of* Jesus His Son.
> (1 John 1:5b–7a VOICE)

What does it look like to walk in God's pure light? In my mind I saw two companioning together: asking, looking, listening, responding to each other. A winding path washed in soft light illuminated just a step or two ahead.

But I had been walking a different way: bent over, squinty-eyed, trying to figure things out by focusing on all that seemed wrong, wanting to fix and make better. In doing so, I had stepped out of God's light. When I set out on my own—to investigate, to uncover, to make sense, to try to influence or change—I began following someone else down a darkened path. I lost fellowship with God by overthinking another's way of seeing, thinking, and acting. That path held hidden dangers. On it I was more susceptible to assumptions and judgments.

Fear, pride, and shame exist on every human path. As I became ultra-focused on James's path, I looked and listened to him more than I looked and listened to God. I inadvertently picked up some of the darkness there, and it lodged in *my* head and heart. We all have enough darkness in our own hearts; we need not borrow it from others. But I absorbed some of my son's, by turning my eyes to him and not to God. And in the dark I got confused.

To walk in the light again, I needed to change direction. How to do this? Instead of trying to figure that out on my own (dark path), I asked God (light path).

In my humanness I wanted this to be black and white, right or wrong, light or dark. That would have made it easier to understand, easier to execute, and given me a perceived sense of control in an out-of-control place. Admittedly, I sometimes wanted to be on the side of light and to cast James on the side of dark. *I* wanted to be the one doing this right. But we were living in a picture with a good amount of gray—unclear and uncertain, with places of mystery, places that were unfinished and in process. A broader view introduced surprising color to our picture: color that blended and softened the black and white, color that held beauty and life. And I wanted to live in the whole picture, not in a black-and-white world. Seeking a way toward life, I asked God, "Have I picked up something in the dark that keeps me in a black-and-white world?"

An old, familiar voice rose to the surface. Its words became clear and sharp. *You are failing. This mess is your fault. Someone else could do this better. You are not enough.* The shadowy figure of shame came out of hiding. And I asked God to forgive me for believing it again.

I sensed that God wanted to supply something new, and so I asked for that—and then listened.

A deeper, more resonant voice whispered, *Juli, you are My pearl.* It surprisingly fit very well.

A good friend and I had recently studied shame together with God. And one insight from that study stayed with me. However, while my brain still recalled it, I hadn't let my heart feel it. I hadn't let it sink in and become something I believed with my whole self and believed for me in the actual events of my life.

Here now, walking in the light, God invited me to more fully and personally receive this: Jesus said that God is "like a jeweler on the lookout for the finest pearls. When he found a pearl more beautiful and valuable than any jewel he had ever seen, the jeweler sold all he had and bought that pearl, *his pearl of great price*" (Matthew 13:45b–46, VOICE). The Jeweler, in fact, purchased the entire field that this treasure was hidden in. This priceless pearl was so sacred and invaluable to the Jeweler that He gave all, even His very life, to recover it. Macrina Wiederkehr explains, "It is pure gift to be able to recognize our littleness as valuable. We are a treasure waiting to be discovered. We are often the very last to discover the treasure of ourselves. You are that treasure, that precious stone."[42]

I am God's pearl of great price. And He bought the whole field of me just as I am, for the treasure that I am and am becoming.

This obscure, ordinary walk in my neighborhood

became a sacred, holy moment where God told me I was His pearl. Mess that I am, small as I feel, I am a treasure to Him. The shame-filled message of "I am wrong, a failure, not enough" melted in the light of the truth that I am, in fact, precious, valuable, honored, and treasured. I don't belong to any who calls me less than that. They have no say over my life at all. God bought me, paid for me; I now belong to Him.

My walk became a celebration with God. Lingering in the joy of this discovery, I mentioned to God that I would love to have a tangible reminder that I am His pearl. I figured it might be helpful to have something to hold when shame mocked and tempted me. A pearl ring, maybe? Arhaus and Sundance have really nice jewelry (wink, wink). And then I laughed. How like a girl to twist a wonderful, spiritual connection into an occasion for new jewelry! And silly, too, to discuss this with God. But I love that our relationship had become free and uninhibited. We could converse about little things, silly things, and everyday things. It was okay to joke with God.

I'm not joking, however, when I tell you that I looked up from these ramblings to see an Arhaus delivery truck in the next driveway. Ha! A random, crazy coincidence? Maybe. But what if God was letting me know I'm not silly? What if He was telling me He'd love to help me remember who I am?

I did get a pearl ring. A friend gave me hers when I shared this story. It's a pretty big pearl, and I wear it when I anticipate a need to remember. It helps me guard my heart and mind. It nudges me to choose the lighted path with God. And this ushers me into a world of color and beauty and life. In that world there is a whisper that is closer than the disparaging voices. It hints that I am His, and only what He says matters.

We are all, each one, a pearl to Him. He sees each of us as a treasure. My jaunts down dark paths of willfully trying to help others see and walk in this light are futile. I can't make someone else see. I can't force connection with them either. But as I walk step by step with God, there is the hope of connection. Ultimately and always, God's best ideas exceed my best ideas. These days I hope you will find me walking more and more in that pure and simple light.

A single lustrous pearl, formed in secret as an irritant finds its way into a clam or oyster. A natural defense mechanism kicks in. Over time, this mysteriously becomes a treasure. Painted by my friend Andrea.

Campfire Conversation
Pearl

1. In which areas of your life do you need light for your path—a next right step or fresh hope in a hard place? Have you shared this with anyone? Where might God be in this?

2. In which areas of your life have you found yourself trapped in black-and-white/right-or-wrong/either-or thinking? How might God want to bring a broader perspective and some color into your way of seeing a person or situation?

3. Do you feel bent over, squinty-eyed, as if you're trying to figure something out? What would it look like to lean back into mystery and unknowing and trust God? How does it feel to shift your posture?

4. Have you ever asked God to help you become aware of shame's voice? What does shame (a sense that something about you is wrong) look like, feel like, and sound like to you? How can we know that shame is not from God, not of God, not intended to be ours?

5. Do you know that you, just as you are, are a treasure to God? Have you let yourself feel this? Have you ever tried to earn or achieve that? Where has that gotten you? What helps you to live in God's affirmation and acceptance as a gift?

_____

_____

_____

_____

_____

_____

_____

_____

_____

_____

_____

_____

_____

_____

10

Boundaries

*L*ong before James joined our family, we were planning for him. My daily request was "God, give me Your heart to love him."

Upon his arrival, as I groped around in my dark heart, I felt fear, guilt, and confusion. But I couldn't find love. In hindsight, I know love was there. I just couldn't feel it. It was buried under many other things.

At the time, I tried harder. I asked more often. But my continued lack of warm feelings only multiplied my fear and triggered shame. What kind of mom was I if I didn't feel love? I'd often heard, "Act in love and your heart will follow," and so I did. But feelings of affection, attachment, and tenderness often still eluded me. Love continued to be a choice and a discipline.

Eventually, with many tears I shared my unmet

request in a counseling session. My counselor responded, "I don't know why God seems to not answer. But maybe it's time to ask Him for something else."

This resonated, and so together we searched for words that framed my need. "Lord, show me where to draw the line" is what emerged. It became my go-to petition, and God answered it time and again.

In the beginning I was hesitant to let go of asking for love. Isn't that what a mother *should* feel? And this new request involved vulnerability and risk. What if God required more of me than I had to give? What if I felt unsafe with where God might draw the lines? Yet I discovered many times that where God led me to establish a boundary gave me more breathing room and gave James healthy limits. In some instances, God invited me farther out, beyond what I thought I could do. But I encountered Him there. He stayed beside me, and we stepped out together.

One of these occasions was an out-of-state visit to James in a residential treatment setting. After several years in our home as we offered all the support we knew to give, James and our relationship with him were unraveling. Determined to not give up, we reached further for help in this residential setting. With high hopes of restoration and a new start, we embraced this tremendous commitment. Frequent visits became part of our rhythm. On this occasion, my husband's work and our family's schedule would not allow us both to travel. A friend suggested I go alone. I laughed at the inconceivable suggestion. She just didn't understand the nature of my relationship with James. I'm the last person James would want to see.

And it felt so unsafe. His anger and the rage that sometimes boiled over to the surface scared me. He knew this and would use it to keep me at a distance, for he, in turn, had things that scared him—things like care and connection. We were both, it seems, running on fear. Over time, the lack of emotional safety took its toll on me, and I began to question my physical safety with him as well. Though nothing concrete had occurred to validate that fear, you couldn't convince my heart of that, so I immediately discounted my friend's idea of visiting him alone. Yet her suggestion echoed in my mind the next morning, so I asked, "God, show me where to draw the line."

Later that day I was in a yoga class. This practice helped me release the overload of tension and stress in my body and experience peace. At the end of class, I was lying on the mat in *savasana*—a pose of letting go and surrendering. James came to mind out of nowhere, and I sensed God inviting me to visit him alone. Tears immediately pooled in my eyes. This was not what I expected. I was weary of putting myself out there and afraid of more rejection. Yet, more than anything I wanted to please God. I really let myself cry on the way home as I surrendered to this invitation. In all honesty I said, "I don't want to, God, but I will if You ask."

As the trip materialized, I felt surprisingly comforted

and less afraid. Arriving at the airport with time to spare, I wandered into a bookstore and noticed a title: *Somewhere Safe with Somebody Good*. An unbidden desire washed over me. *I wish I were going somewhere safe with somebody good.*

On its heels came a gentle correction*: No, I am. I am going somewhere safe with Somebody good.* God had invited me on this trip. This was an adventure with Him.

And that's precisely what I discovered. The time with James was challenging. He remained largely unavailable and closed-off. But God showed up in unexpected ways. He provided me with the courage to be fully present. He opened the way for good connections with others. And He illuminated sticky situations that exposed the reality of where we were relationally. These were not easy truths to see, but they helped us navigate a way forward.

Meanwhile, the work of boundaries continued. God was teaching me through resources and shaping me by the opportunities to put those into practice. The resources, however, were not a precise formula. As Dallas Willard explains, "We are not told in any systematic way how to do our part in the process. Well, at least we are not told in precise terms—certainly not in formulas. This is because the process [of transformation and growth] is to be a walk with a person."[43] Here are some of the teachings I walked out with God:

The most compassionate people I interviewed also have the most well-defined and well-respected boundaries. It surprised me at the time, but now I get it. They assume that other people are doing the best they can, but they also ask for what they need, and they don't put up with a lot of crap. I lived the opposite way: I assumed that people weren't doing their best, so I judged them and constantly fought being disappointed, which was easier than setting boundaries. Boundaries are hard when you want to be liked and when you are a pleaser hell-bent on being easy, fun, and flexible. Compassionate people ask for what they need. They say no when they need to, and when they say yes, they mean it. They're compassionate because their boundaries keep them out of resentment. (Brené Brown, *Rising Strong*)[44]

Hurt and harm are different. . . . You need to evaluate the effects of setting boundaries and be responsible to the other person, but that does not mean you should avoid setting boundaries because someone responds with hurt or anger. . . . Deciding to set boundaries is difficult because it requires decision making and confrontation,

> which, in turn, may cause pain to someone
> you love. We need to evaluate the pain
> caused by our making choices and empa-
> thize with it. We need to see how this hurt
> is helpful to others and sometimes the best
> thing we can do for them and the relation-
> ship. (Cloud and Townsend, *Boundaries*)[45]

Amazingly, as I let go of what I felt an obligation to pray ("Give me Your love for him") and picked up the more accessible prayer ("Show me where to draw the line"), God answered. I discovered deeper truths regarding love: drawing lines and establishing boundaries were, in fact, the building blocks of love. Love sometimes looked like saying no in ways that caused hurt. Bound-aries created healthy conditions for love to take root and grow. Boundaries supported me to love in difficult circumstances.

God had not ignored my pleas. He had been answer-ing my prayer all along to love James as He loves James. Part of the process involved letting go of blind, enabling ways of love, which are ultimately more focused on me looking and feeling good. He taught me a better way to love, with "knowledge and depth of insight" (Philippians 1:9b NIV). In this way, love would multiply and increase. I no longer needed to fear losing it or hoard it as a scarce commodity. Living into this deeper wisdom, love "will overflow more and more" (Philippians 1:9a NLT).

On this journey I encountered the temptation to let voices of fear set boundaries instead of God. I learned by trial and error to distinguish those voices. Fear caused me to feel unsettled, pressured, panicky, hurried, or frenzied. God's voice stretched me, but His invitations were always accompanied by some good gift like courage or energy or peace. There was also breathing room along the way with God. I never experienced Him as being in a hurry.

A song in Scripture describes the beauty and fruit of trusting God with my boundaries: "The Lord is my chosen portion and my cup; you hold my lot. The lines have fallen for me in pleasant places; indeed, I have a beautiful inheritance" (Psalm 16:5–6 ESV).

This song goes on to describe the inheritance that lies within God's boundaries. For my family, and for me, these borders hold refuge, delight, counsel, rest, safety, stability, joy, every good thing, guidance, godly people, true heroes, and pleasures forevermore. Therefore, "I will bless the Eternal, whose wise teaching orches- trates my days and centers my mind at night. He is ever present with me; *at all times He goes before me.* I will not live in fear *or abandon my calling* because He stands at my right hand" (Psalm 16:7–8 VOICE) . . . and shows me where to draw the line.

Along the way I also learned that adoption *is* in love: "In love he predestined us for adoption to himself" (Ephesians 1:4b–5a ESV). When we are partnering with Him, love isn't something we add to adoption. If His love were an ocean, adoption would be immersed within its waters. "In love" is where God has located adoption and what God has for us in adoption. Love is the birthplace, the context, and it's enough because it's God's supply of love, not just my own. I didn't need to strive for it. It was already there. I just needed to learn to establish boundaries that allow for the love that is there to surface and flourish and do its good work.

> [In] our material creation, boundaries mark the most beautiful of places, between the ocean and the shore, between the mountains and the plains, where the canyon meets the river. [God] will teach you to thrill with [Him] in the boundaries while you learn to trust [Him] with your security and safety. (William P. Young, *Cross Roads*)[46]

Lord, may these boundaries that I have set to the best of my ability and in trust with You become beautiful—like some of my most favorite places shared with people I love . . .

Trail 6 at Turkey Run State Park, a boundary of canyon cliffs, separating the creek bed in the valley from the bright forest above.

Lake Michigan at Indiana Dunes State Park, a boundary of earth and sky and sea—and a really fun place to play.

Venture Out Park at St. Andrews Bay, the boundary of night and day that we call sunrise reflecting its light on the quiet water of early morning.

Sunset on our boat dock at Lake Lanier, a boundary of water, earth, and sky that constantly changes, so we all watch with rapt attention.

Sunset Point at Turkey Run State Park, a boundary of day and night over the water of Sugar Creek. My mom and I timed our hike perfectly to catch this.

Campfire Conversation
Boundaries

1. Is there a prayer you have prayed for a long time with no sense of God responding? What might it look like to search for a new prayer in that situation? What hesitations do you have with that? How might you let the old prayer rest with God so you can pick up something new, something more within reach?

2. Have you ever been "running on fear" (where fear is the voice that drives you and motivates your actions and responses)? What is fear telling you? How might God respond to that voice? Perhaps it's not fear as much as pride? What might pride be telling you? And how do you imagine God would respond to that voice?

3. What do you perceive as the difference between drawing boundary lines and putting up walls? When have you put up a wall? When have you drawn a line? What have you learned in these spaces?

4. What stands out to you in the Brené Brown quote? In the Cloud and Townsend quote? Is there an invitation for you in either of these? A way to grow in compassion and/or wisdom?

5. Where might you ask God to help you love "with knowledge and depth of insight"? How can you make some space for Him to respond to that request?

6. What are some of your favorite boundary places? What do you love most about them?

_____

_____

_____

_____

_____

_____

_____

_____

_____

_____

_____

_____

_____

11

Puzzles

My husband and I are currently into a British crime drama on Netflix. I mostly enjoy it, but whenever they play slow, haunting music, signaling that something bad is about to happen, I leave the room. I often keep watching, but only from a safe distance.

A similar type of dread-inducing music has been playing in my head in the background of my days. I've tried leaving the room. Without success, I've attempted to outrun, outperform, and outmaneuver it. It's only become more explicit in the form of a word—a pesky word. I kinda choke up trying to say it out loud . . . *fail*.

That's the word. It scares me. So I've attempted to ignore it, stuff it, starve it, even deal with it—or so I thought. I've thrown all my resources at it: a lot of time, money, and sacrifices. Yet it just gets louder and closer.

I really thought Jesus and I had worked through this. Surely we tackled the guilt, blame, and shame—this baggage of failure. Then the first line of the first song in a Sunday morning church service refers to failure as a friend.[47]

Ugh.

A month ago someone close said serious things to me that struck the bull's-eye of this failure. The message I heard was "You aren't loving enough. You aren't giving enough. You *aren't* enough. I'm disappointed in you." It hurt in a breathless, stunning way.

And then God delivered layer upon layer of deep comfort. He first comforted me in the form of my mom . . . who just listened. When she spoke, she told me I wasn't disappointing to her; then we enjoyed the gift of really sweet time together with good food, lighthearted movies, and jigsaw puzzles. I loved working on jigsaw puzzles with my mom. Conversation was light. We were quiet together too. No agenda intruded our space but to fit pieces of a puzzle together one at a time. And somehow, while putting pieces of a puzzle together, God fit some pieces together in me. I realized that disappointing others was inevitable, as was the reality of others disappointing me. In hindsight, *I survived that*. Failure caught up with me. Disappointment caught up with me. And yet I am still here.

And God is too.

My mind tells me that failure is shameful and isolating. But my experience has been that in failure, Jesus

154

moves closer. I wrestled with the stigma of it and the outward appearance until I wore myself out. Then failure invited me in. What I mean is, I discovered that my real work wasn't striving to make things look more successful on the outside. Instead, God gave me permission to let failure be what it was so I could look for Him within it. It was a season to work inside, not outside.

Thomas Keating, an author and priest, describes this season in our spiritual lives looking like "darkness, spiritual dryness, and confusion."[48] In these places, he says, "We think that God has abandoned us. . . . We think that God must have departed for the next universe and couldn't care less about us. [But] . . . Instead of going away, God simply moves downstairs, so to speak, and waits for us to come and join him."[49]

This inward journey, as some call it, began in the place of my failure. I let go of striving to change that and began to find God in practices like silence and solitude, meditation, contemplation, and spiritual direction. Finding God in these places began to change my understanding of self and my image of God. I am still discovering that He is more deeply, thoroughly good than I ever dreamed possible—than I could ever, ever put into words.

Many books describe individuals' inward journeys with God. But if I settled for secondhand learning, I would miss out on *my* unique and personal journey with God. There was a cost, however. It cost me my reputation and productivity. It cost me disappointing others. And it cost me the appearance of "success." Whatever its price, it is thoroughly worthwhile. Thomas Keating says, "The spiritual journey is not a career or a success story. It is a series of humiliations of the false self that become more and more profound. These make room inside of us for the Holy Spirit to come in and heal. What prevents us from being available to God is gradually evacuated. We keep getting closer and closer to our center."[50] But this time, in contrast to the breathless pain of when others try to dissect what's underneath, when God touches this center we find healing and movement toward wholeness.

So yes, failure has sought to be my friend. And I'm learning not to be afraid of it. In fact, I'm discovering God *in* it. God even speaks in the Bible about seasons of external barrenness. Amazingly, there *is* fruit there, in the seemingly empty land. I just don't immediately recognize it because it grows gradually from the inside out.

Fully developed, it looks like joy, strength, bravery, and spiritual progress.

> Though the fig tree does not blossom and there is no fruit on the vines, [though] the product of the olive fails and the fields yield no food, though the flock is cut off from the fold and there are no cattle in the stalls, Yet I will *rejoice* in the Lord; I will exult in the [victorious] God of my salvation! The Lord God is my *Strength*, my personal *bravery*, and

> my invincible army; He makes my feet like
> hinds' feet and will make me to walk [not to
> stand still in terror, but to walk] and make
> [*spiritual*] *progress* upon my high places
> [of trouble, suffering, or responsibility]!
> (Habakkuk 3:17–19, AMPC, emphasis mine)

I once imagined these words being barked out in a robust, military-like instruction—a steely determination of "I *will* be joyful! I *will* be strong!" Now I picture it like this: I stop trying to fix what seems disappointing and weak in me. Letting that be, I can turn to look inside. Almost with surprise, I discover, there's joy! I didn't put that here. And there's strength! I didn't manufacture that either. Picking up these fruits within, I let them nourish me. I live from the resources I discover, not the resources I think I'm supposed to make happen.

Returning to the song that began my Sunday morning, I find more. While the world either judges failure and barks improvement orders or excuses it and blames others, God offers something different. There is an alternative, another place to go with my failure: the cross. By all appearances, it was Jesus's worst failure on display. Yet below and beyond the surface, it was God covering the cost of all our collective failures and freeing us from that shame, guilt, and fear. Jesus's last words on the cross, "It is finished" (John 19:30b NRSV), echo God's final words in Scripture, "It is done" (Revelation 21:6b NRSV). This is what heaven says, what the ultimate Judge declares regarding failure. Essentially, "I've covered it." And who doesn't need coverage for his or her shortcomings and waywardness?

"It is done." I had been looking for a response to my accusers, knowing it had to come from Jesus. I couldn't adequately defend myself. I'd been waiting to hear what He would say. And I now realized, He's already said it. "It is done," He reminds me. Such a simple, powerful response. Such a final reply in the face of all past, present, and future accusations. It ends the argument, ends the conversation—including those internal ones continuously circling my head. He hands me this, and it feels something like the satisfaction of fitting the final piece into a big, beautiful puzzle—only better.

My puzzle partner in a favorite sunny spot.

Campfire Conversation
Puzzles

1. What comes to mind for you with the word *fail*? What feelings does it evoke in you?

2. What has been your experience of God in the midst of failure? How do you differentiate between God, others, and yourself in these spaces? Whose voice is loudest? What is it saying?

3. What would it look like for you to seek God in dark (scary or unknown), dry (weary), or confusing (unclear) places? What do openness and surrender to God look like here?

4. How do you attempt to distance yourself from failure? In contrast, where have you let failure get close enough to be a companion, a teacher, a friend to you? What have you discovered there?

5. What do you think God might want to offer you in place of your failure? Could you ask Him for something? Are you open to receiving from Him in that vulnerable place? Why or why not?

6. When God says, "It is done," what do you think that means? What might it mean for you personally?

What does it look like, applied to your particular life and circumstances? Is there a chance that God's picture is bigger or better than you imagined or have been told? Have you/can you ask Him what He intends and means for you?

Fields

My husband and I have different approaches to some things, like the garbage. When the can naturally reaches its capacity, I like to take it out. My husband, on the other hand, will stuff it down, making more room for more garbage. He can endlessly find more space. I'm not a fan. An overfull bag is hard to remove and likely to break. Picking up spilled garbage stinks. So if the can is full, let's just take it out.

Garbage tends to accumulate beyond the kitchen as well. My heart is a container sometimes for rotted things like anger, resentment, and finding fault. In a particularly messy season, my heart work was to forgive. I approached this as a task, like taking out the kitchen garbage. It's unpleasant work, but it needs to be done, so let's "git 'er done," as my son likes to say. In my efforts to forgive, I saw God's role as looking over my shoulder, noting the heart garbage, and admonishing me to get to it.

I pursued forgiveness as a studied act of obedience, researching and reading books, trying to sort out a way forward. Unforgiveness was an enemy of my heart and I found what I wanted: a formula to deal it a fatal blow.

The problem was that it kept coming back. So I reread the book, and more—I *lived into* the book with God. I was grateful to have a checklist to navigate something so intangible, vague, and ominous. Journaling became a way of working the formula, pouring out my heart, my need, and my lack onto the page.

Looking back I see that this alone didn't affect lasting change, and expecting a certain outcome from the process was hard on my soul. During this time, someone close asked me in a defensive posture, "Have you forgiven James?" I reeled inwardly at the accusation. Was this God's question too?

"I'm trying my best," I said.

But the interaction heaped on shame. And all the while, I was learning through experience that these things can't be forced or formulated. As much as I wished otherwise, I couldn't just take out this garbage. Forgiveness was a mystery to me, an elusive shadow I could not apprehend.

In hindsight, I see that the issue wasn't so much the process I followed, but that I was looking to and relying on a process instead of God. King David from the Bible became a mentor, teaching me what it looked like to focus on God and not on the task or formula. I learned the ancient practice of lament—a way to be with the painful and hard *with* God. David's songs of lament gave me permission to complain and language to name my enemies and share my feelings of hurt, anger, and fear. As opposed to my earlier efforts to seize and master forgiveness, I was learning to show up and cooperate in the uncomfortable work of being honest and transparent—and not as a means to an end but as a place to be with God.

Forgiveness, I discovered, is a process much like grief. It happens in stages, and no journey is identical. Rather than making it happen, I could only attend to where I was and be there with Jesus. When I sensed Jesus present with the enemies in my heart, they began to lose their power, and I found myself more open to creative solutions and the energy to engage.

I learned it's okay to be in denial; that's a stage of forgiveness. I practiced finding the gift in anger, to honor it by listening to it. Writing letters helped. Mostly they were letters that in the end I did not send. But I sensed Jesus with me as I wrote. In one bout of anger, I wrote what I thought was articulate, clear, and convincing. I held that letter with Jesus but eventually sensed it would likely not achieve our shared desire to reconcile the relationship or mend the situation. So I let it go.

The urge to make things right didn't die so easily. With fresh inspiration, I wrote another letter from a different angle. Yet again, I recognized the same probable result. Disheartened as I walked down a quiet hallway at church, I paused at a framed photograph. The image set Jesus in a modern-day context. Sitting on the front steps of what appears to be a place of business, Jesus gazes out thoughtfully and at rest. A businessman, dressed for success, has laid his head on Jesus's lap and fallen asleep. His briefcase is open before him with papers scattered here and there—one still clutched loosely in his hand. Somehow this captured me and all the letters. I was exhausted with my best efforts. And Jesus was right there, inviting me to let go and rest. He knew the complexities of the situation. He knew my desire to connect and reconcile. He was asking me to rest my head, my heart, and this quandary with Him. When my best words fell short and I was worn out, Jesus offered me a place to stop trying. I was finally ready to do that. This image with my Friend, Jesus, was such a far cry from a demanding God, commanding me to forgive and reconcile right now. And it more closely aligned with the God I've encountered on this journey—a God who is with me in the exhaustion of my own efforts, not in a hurry, and not without hope.

In another bout of my anger, a counselor asked me to list the reasons I was mad, itemizing all that felt lost or taken from my family and me. It was a long list. Then she asked me to add a second column with the heading "Why?" She wanted me to name where my anger likely came from. I immediately felt uneasy and frustrated—

resistant to this step. My answers to each line were identical. This maddening trait or situation existed due to early-life trauma and circumstances beyond my son's control. As I shifted from column one to column two, the blame I had directed toward him shifted into blame directed toward myself. In attempting to make sense of our chaotic circumstances, my rational brain told me that if it wasn't his fault that our home was a wreck, then it must be mine. Blame became shame, and the heaviness felt unbearable.

I wanted to burn my list but took it home instead. And God surprised me with a sweet remedy, something that covered and canceled both columns, all the blame and all the shame. With a big green Sharpie, I wrote it over the top of this inventory:

So now the case is closed. There remains no accusing voice of condemnation against those who are joined in life-union with Jesus . . . [who] gave his body to be the sin-offering so that God could once and for all condemn the guilt and power of sin. . . . And we are free to live, not according to our flesh, but by the dynamic power of the Holy Spirit! . . . [and] the mind-set controlled by the Spirit finds life and peace." (Romans 8:1a, 3b, 4b, 6b TPT)

Instead of sentencing either of us with these losses and offenses, God sentenced the guilt, blame, and shame itself. He took those on Himself and offered us freedom and peace. A huge weight (times two) lifted off me, and I learned to live more and more into freedom. As the accusing voices of blame and shame became more distinct and recognizable, God gave me permission to ignore them. More than that, He warned me: refuse to engage in their conversation. When they pulled on me, I saw in my mind's eye the canceled list of offenses instead.

This realization gradually freed my heart and mind, and I became more aware of James living in his own prison of blame and shame. Similar lists with columns of offense, accusation, and fault held him captive in steel bars. After some years, an opportunity came to share with him what I had learned and experienced with God. I sought to invite him into his own journey of forgiveness, freedom, life, and peace. I tried, but it seemed out of reach. And there was permission for him to write his own letters and list his own complaints, do whatever helped him express his pain. Jesus would wait for him, too, to lay it all down and turn around.

That commonly used church word *repent* means to "turn around." I used to picture it as if God were an intimidating old man pointing His large, crooked finger in my face and, with a furrowed brow, grumbling a low "Repent, sinner!"

But my experience was decidedly different. I had come to know God as a Friend at my back, leaning in to whisper, "Turn around. I'm behind you. Life is in My direction." In my imagination, I turn to see Jesus, His arms spread wide, welcoming me home. Beyond Him I catch a glimpse of the more to come, ground we will cover together in time. James had his own ground to cover, his own turning points to make. My words and efforts did not seem to help him. Yet my personal journey of forgiveness continued.

There was a beautiful day at the beach. It was my birthday, and I paused, reflecting on this back-and-forth, roundabout path of forgiveness. Far from giving me an evaluation or report card, God pointed to the progress we'd made and the ground we had covered together. Better yet, there was more to come. Jesus and I celebrated both good things. We embraced the freedom to be where I was and anticipated greater freedom yet to come. I knew I hadn't "arrived." We couldn't check the box or respond to my friend's accusation with "Yes, I have forgiven him!" Not all the garbage had been taken out. But this was where I was supposed to be. And I wasn't there alone. A deep sense of peace settled over me.

I eventually came to a choice: to renew or release my relationship with James. This choice arrived in the form of a picture. Desmond Tutu and his daughter Mpho Tutu in *The Book of Forgiving* used the image of a field to represent this relationship, the place of possibility, and the decision at hand. My field was newly plowed and cleared of debris and weeds. Its boundaries were now well-defined.

As I stood with God at its borders, it appeared to be just a lot of brown mud. But much work had been done. I'd poured sweat, tears, and time into it. And here it sat, empty.

But empty was work. Empty was potential. And empty it would need to remain for now. It was not the right season to plant new seeds of relationship, and nothing else could grow in this field. This relationship was unique. This individual could not be replaced. It was a bittersweet moment. Soon after, so unexpectedly and painfully, two fallow fields appeared in my life—not what I wanted. In that second relationship I asked the other party to meet and work with me, but they were not ready. I sat with the Lord by these fields, really sad. I sensed Him speaking to my heart:

This is a season to leave the fields fallow. You have permission, even as an act of obedience, to put the tools down and turn around and walk away. Working and working this soil isn't going to change it. It's only breaking your back and shoulders, leaving you with knotted muscles, pain, and exhaustion. I'm sorry you have two fallow fields. It's okay to cry. It fits to be sad. Share that with Me. Acknowledge this loss. It's not what you wanted.

And then—turn around. There are other fields ripe and plentiful. Check out their fruit.

Taste and enjoy. Work in these other fields. Walk among them. I am with you, so be all here. Lean in with your full weight.

I will let you know if/when/how to give attention back to the fallow fields. I won't let you miss it. For now we will guard the borders we cleared together. If weeds of unforgiveness, resentment, or fear pop back up, we'll pull them out together. In the meantime, refrain from thinking and talking about them. Resist the urge to question, imagine, speculate, or brainstorm ways to improve or change the soil conditions. Instead, feast and feed others from the fruitful fields I have given you. Receive those blessings.

When you are hyper-attuned, listening for activity from the fallow fields, replaying their voices in your mind, it prevents you from hearing all the ways and places I'm saying, "Well done, Juli." Turn around and tune your ears to Me. Receive all I'm telling you. Feast on my faithfulness; there is plenty in this season.

It's been said that our spiritual formation (our transformation from the inside out to become like Jesus) is the slowest of all processes on the face of the earth. Forgiveness, likewise, is slow work and in many ways still a mystery to me. I'm more comfortable now letting it be what it is, allowing myself to be where I am, and letting others be where they are. This world, even the religious part of it sometimes, has conditioned me to expect instant relationship, instant answers from God, instant forgiveness, and instant growth and maturity. In sharp contrast, God encourages me to take one step at a time, reassuring me that it's good to grow into my life little by little.

Ultimately, this isn't about garbage. It's about the fields that lie below and beyond all that debris. These fields hold such potential to nourish and be enjoyed. So whenever garbage starts piling, instead of trying to take it out or stuff it down, I've found this to be the best starting place of all:

I want to be willing to forgive
But I dare not ask for the will to forgive
in case you give it to me
and I am not yet ready
I am not yet ready to be vulnerable again
Not yet ready to see that there is humanity
in my tormenter's eyes

Or that the one who hurt me
may also have cried
I am not yet ready for the journey
I am not yet interested in the path
I am at the prayer before the
prayer of forgiveness

I don't know that I ever appreciated the beauty of a fallow field until Andrea painted it.

Campfire Conversation
Fields

1. Is your tendency to stuff something or fix it? Maybe some of both? Is there an area of your life in which you are doing that now? How is that hard on your soul? What might God want to offer as another way (a third way) forward?

2. Where has forgiveness intersected with your life? Where are you now with that? How does it feel to be there? What do the voices of blame and/or shame say? In contrast, how do you (or do you) sense God present there?

3. Are there any "fallow fields" (relationships that you are not currently investing in because they are not safe) in your life? How do you feel about them? What is your desire for them? What questions do you have? Have you/can you share this with God?

4. Where have you exhausted your own efforts for now? What would it look like for you to rest with God where you are? How are rest and trust similar? What might God want to offer you there? What do you think is the difference between resting in the unfinished and stuffing/avoiding something?

5. Where might God be whispering, "Turn around"?
   Where might life be found in a different direction
   than the one you are facing? What keeps you from
   "repenting"?

_____

_____

_____

_____

_____

_____

_____

_____

_____

_____

_____

_____

_____

_____

Blessed

A particular word makes an appearance everywhere. It seems overused to me, maybe
thoughtlessly tossed about. "Have a blessed day." "I'm
so blessed." And even the ubiquitous, online "#blessed."

I've wondered if anyone really knows what that
means. Clothing is blessed. Towels are blessed. Pillows
are blessed. You name it. We've blessed everyone and
everything, and we (I think) have no idea of what we're
really saying.

Recently, however, someone reintroduced me to
blessed. It began at a retreat center outside of Chicago.
The days were long and full of learning. Our only break
was two hours in the late afternoon. In that time I would
flee for the outdoors, drinking in fresh air, quiet space,
and room to move. I'd fill every minute of those precious

hours walking around a lake until the bells chimed six. Early in the week I noticed an obscure side path made of stepping stones. Curious, I followed it to the edge of the woods and found a beautiful mosaic of Mary, the mother of Jesus, ornately framed and standing among a grove of pine trees. I studied it and found myself drawn to her heart: full, flesh-colored, healthy. Most strikingly, it was pierced by swords all around.

The image stayed with me as I continued to walk. Slowly, a connection with the swords surfaced. I too had raw, painful places—personal experiences of rejection and inadequacy, and my boys' recent struggles that, as their mom, I felt with them. Mary's exposed pain resonated. Swords *can* pierce a mother's heart.

I continued to walk with thoughts of Mary. Despite her swords, she seemed healthy, whole, and strong. I later picked up her story in Scripture. Right away I saw it: *blessed*. As I read her story, I traced a literal trail of blessings. An angel planted the first seed: "Rejoice, highly favored *one*, the Lord *is* with you; blessed *are* you among women!" (Luke 1:28b NKJV). And then her Aunt Elizabeth confirmed, "Blessed *are* you among women" (Luke 1:42b NKJV). The mosaic embodied this word.

I wondered if Mary felt *blessed*. I wondered if she even knew what the word meant. Did it resonate with her? Intrigued, I began to study it. Its definition was mostly what I expected: "well-off, fortunate, the nature of that which is the highest good."[53] The surprise came in the circumstances where it was used.

Aunt Elizabeth is one who really pours it on: "bless you" and "bless your baby" and "blessed is she who believed that there would be a fulfillment of what was spoken to her by the Lord" (Luke 1:45 NRSV). With this last blessing, she is essentially telling Mary, "What makes you most well-off is that you believe, to the point that you act in trust that God will do what He's said He would do." Here was the deepest and purest blessing. It wasn't Mary's upstanding character or the baby that Elizabeth pointed to as the source of blessing. It was Mary's trust. Elizabeth basically said, "What allows you to experience God's highest good is that you rely on Him."

Mary responded with "My soul magnifies the Lord" (Luke 1:46b NRSV), essentially saying, "All I see is God. I've lost sight of the surface of things, the worldly concerns that grasp to control me, the fear and doubt that bully me into living small. And as I lock eyes with God, I see that He sees me. He sees my neediness, humiliation, and mess. He regards the scorn, shame, and threats upon my life." And precisely here, in what she called her "lowliness" or "low places," God lifted her chin and pronounced, "You are blessed, Mary."

Deep within Mary, this resonated as true. So she joined in. "I am blessed," she said out loud, echoing the words spoken as her act of accepting the blessing. Mary tended to her soul by noticing and receiving the blessedness of low places. I wonder if there was a hint of surprise in her voice. Because really, who would think that low places hold blessing?

Years later, Jesus gave further meaning to this word. He recited a list of who is blessed, and how that is, in the discourse we know now as the Sermon on the Mount. In his book *The Divine Conspiracy*, Dallas Willard notes how our human nature, bent toward performing, achieving, and controlling, is tempted to make these Beatitudes *conditions* for blessedness. But Jesus isn't saying, "Be like this." He isn't setting a bar. These are not "if you do this, then you are blessed" statements.[54] Instead, each is a "no matter what" statement—"no matter what messy, needy, broken shape you are currently in, I see you. And I am here, and My Kingdom and all its resources are available to you. That's why you are blessed." It's exactly what Mary had discovered years earlier. Jesus in these statements breaks it down further, naming specifically some of the low places of blessing.

To begin, He says, "Blessed are the poor in spirit, for theirs is the kingdom of heaven" (Matthew 5:3 NRSV). I imagine Jesus looking out into this crowd of ordinary, common, uneducated people. He makes eye contact with someone who feels inadequate in His company and the crowd of religious elite He draws. And He sees that person's low place and says, "Blessed are those without a wisp of religion or spiritual qualifications . . . the ones with no religious glitter or clout. The whole kingdom of heaven belongs to them" (Dallas Willard).[55] He wasn't complimenting those who had achieved humility. He was calling out to the uneducated nobodies. This wasn't an academic lecture with an exhaustive list of instructions to achieve blessedness. Jesus was looking into the faces and, more so, the souls around Him, and speaking blessing to real conditions and messy lives. On that day He proved He saw them, even the insides of them. And with that, I think they believed He could bless them even there.

Because Jesus's list was not exhaustive and, in fact, couldn't be exhausted, Dallas encouraged his students to write their own beatitudes. The assignment was *Find where the blessing meets my life*. This is what Mary did with her low places. In getting specific about what felt lacking and uncertain, she discovered an invitation to live with Jesus in that very place. He was there with His resources, power, and love. She didn't have to get herself cleaned up, educated, happier, or more thankful, optimistic, or humble. She didn't need to improve something first. Thus, in my own family crisis or health crisis, or whatever is going on, Jesus is here too, with the resources of the kingdom of God.

Naming my own beatitudes wasn't easy, but defining my hard places led to a discovery of particular resources in the kingdom of heaven for exactly that place.

My beatitudes:

- *Blessed are those whose lives feel small and in danger, reduced and threatened by anxiety, for theirs are the vast resources and energy of the kingdom of heaven.*

- *Blessed are the rejected ones, for they have a place of true and secure belonging as children of God.*
- *Blessed are those who are out of place and disconnected, who long for God in community, for they will be filled in surprising ways, personally, by God. They will know an intimacy with God that few experience.*

I took many more laps around the lake that week away . . . these steps shaping my own trail of blessings. Pausing occasionally at the mosaic of Mary, I noticed new things each visit. Once I observed her hands. They appeared to be reaching out. Bestowing a blessing maybe?

During that week, retreat leaders encouraged us to meet with a spiritual director, someone trained in listening and discernment—noticing God and His presence in our lives. It is a form of soul care, a spiritual practice. Honestly, I almost skipped this. I had lots of good-sounding excuses: "It's something I already do regularly. I'm tired and just wanted to be alone with God. I don't know what to talk about."

But the more excuses I have for not doing something, the more I probably need it. So I showed up. And our conversation unexpectedly revisited a relationship in which I had already done a lot of work. I described an urge to reach out again to the person I had this relationship with. I wondered if that was from God. It became clear as we met that this urge was more of a compulsion in me trying to please, appease, and gain approval.

It wasn't coming from God.

At the end of our session, the spiritual director asked to pray for me. Her prayer came in the form of speaking blessing over me. At one point she said, "I bless you as a _____," naming my relational role with the person I was striving to please. There was a weight to these words. They fit into an empty, needy place. It felt as if God Himself was blessing me in that role. And truly, I think He was.

Mary's outstretched hands of blessing comforted and empowered me. I realized that God had the capacity, the ability, and the authority to bless me in any relational role. And with His blessing, I'm freed from needing any other person's blessing. A new awareness surfaced that this other person was not capable of blessing me. But God could fill that gap, so I did not need something that person could not provide.

Receiving God's blessing in this relationship has been healing, freeing, and empowering. I gradually stopped hiding, making excuses, or trying to prove myself. Though I still felt sad, I no longer needed anything from them. I had done what I could toward fostering a healthy, trustworthy relationship. The remaining gaps were not mine to fill. In this broken relationship, I found another place of blessing, of blessedness.

On one of my last laps around the lake, I took in Mary's colorful robe and the crown on her head. The word "glorious" came to mind.

Mary's circumstances and pain seemed the opposite of glorious: an unaccountable pregnancy, a humble manger, a shameful cross—not so glorious in human, worldly terms. How many times did she feel exposed and raw, inadequate, weak, and alone?

Yet God clothed Mary. He covered her shame again and again. He told her, and she echoed: *These very places of lack are my places of blessing*. She stood before me with her head held high, no shame in her heart, bestowing a similar blessing upon me.

There is a painting by Mariotto Albertinelli of the encounter between Mary and Elizabeth that I love. I love how close they are. I love how earnestly Elizabeth is searching Mary out. Seeking her eyes, she wants Mary to receive the blessing, believe it, and be reassured that in a scary, uncertain, unfamiliar place, *you are blessed*.

God came that close to me too and whispered His personal and insistent reassurance: *Juli, you are blessed— not because you handled this situation flawlessly or because you are a perfect person. You are blessed because I am here, and I desire to work My highest good in your weakness and loss.*

I could no longer ignore the word *blessed*. It was no longer vague or generic. Now it was very personal, and I knew exactly where it fit: in the most unlikely and need-iest of places. Occasions remain when I need to return, remember, and receive it again. *Yes, Lord, I am blessed. Thank You for reminders on towels and t-shirts, pillows and walls. Write this also on my heart, that I might always know.*

The mosaic of Mary by the lake. She became a friend I returned to again and again. Her heart, her hands, and her crown taught me: I am blessed.

Mariotto Albertinelli's *Visitation* painting.[56] Aunt Elizabeth wanting a vulnerable Mary to really, really know that she *is* blessed. I also see in this painting the neediness of Mary and how God welcomes and covers that.

Campfire Conversation
Blessed

1. What does *blessed* mean to you? What memories, feelings, people, or situations come to mind? Do you see God present in those places? How so? Are there certain situations or memories that seem far removed from *blessed*? What would you exclude? Why? Do you see God present in those places?

2. Is there a biblical person or story you particularly connect with that has been a guide for you? How do you relate to it/him or her? What have you learned from it/that person? If you don't relate to one, maybe ask God for this, and then put yourself in a position to listen to and receive what He may offer you.

3. Take up Dallas Willard's assignment and write (with God) your own beatitudes. Find where the blessing meets your life in a place of uncertainty or lack. Make this a practice of prayer, a place of conversation, a back-and-forth with God, as opposed to coming up with these by yourself based on what you know about God. Maybe you have more than one beatitude right now. Begin by asking God, "Where is my place of blessing?" Make space to listen and wait for His response. Also ask God, "What resource is available

in the kingdom of heaven to meet me in this place of need?"

4. Where do you need *God's* blessing? Said another way: Where are you looking for/waiting on/striving for someone else's blessing and approval? Have you/can you ask God for this? Then give Him time to respond.

_____

_____

_____

_____

_____

_____

_____

_____

_____

_____

_____

14

Glasses

I laid my glasses carefully among other items accumulating on the center table. Then I explained to my friends who were circled around this makeshift altar, "I've brought an old pair of my glasses to describe where I am with God these days. I recently came through a tough season. But despite my progress, it seems fear and sadness took hold and distort how I see and respond in the current season. I think if God would show me where He was in the midst of that trial, I could live more freely, lightly, and at peace here and now. These glasses represent my request, 'God, give me eyes to see how You were with us.'"

This was at the beginning of a week-long residency in spiritual formation.

The culmination of this week, spent in lectures and various group learning spaces, was a twenty-four-hour silent retreat. I loved the time away in this idyllic setting outside of Chicago, surrounded by natural beauty, with deep and safe friends. But being an introvert, I found that my favorite part was always the quiet day at the end of the retreat. I crashed into it, tired and needy for silence, space, fresh air, and long walks around the lake.

During one of those walks, I remembered my desire to see God in my difficult past. Right then a phrase randomly popped into my head: "The Holy Ghost over the bent world broods."[57] A new friend had recently introduced me to a beloved poet, Gerard Manley Hopkins. His enjoyment of creation was contagious, and I began spending time with the poet's work myself. This line from his poem "God's Grandeur" describes God creating beauty and goodness out of nothingness and chaos (see Genesis 1). And it hints at His ongoing work of renewing creation when it (we, I) feels like nothing but chaos.

Hopkins's words were a doorway, and within them I imagined God hovering over my family's brokenness in the most demanding places of that season. He leaned into our chaos and sadness—a shielding presence as we grieved the necessity of letting go. And ultimately, slowly, He began to birth something new from it. This was God, responding to my request to see. And what I saw was His "brooding" over our "bent" and broken forms. God responded to my request with more than just a sharper focus. The "glasses" He offered framed this situation in His love. A lens of love allowed me to see the past well.

When we see through love, we grasp what's most real in our circumstances.

Six months later, I was in this retreat setting again. At my first opportunity I headed out around the lake. A surprise waited for me on a favorite bench. There lay a pair of heart-shaped glasses and I smiled, remembering the glasses I had brought to the last residency. Maybe God was reminding me of the lens of love that brought clarity and allowed fear and sadness to lose their hold. I didn't realize there was more.

That week Julian of Norwich captivated me. In lectures I learned about her life during the Middle Ages and the visions of love God gave her. The week flew by, and just before our closing silent retreat, I opened up with a few friends about a place of self-doubt that had recently been triggered. The day before in what I thought to be a safe relationship, I shared vulnerable details of our messy situation. And the other party responded with ill-fitting advice that revealed her lack of understanding. I could have shut down altogether and retreated within myself. But I felt a nudge to open to this group. So I gave voice to the question now swirling inside, "Is this my fault?"

Honestly, I couldn't believe I was here again, doubting myself, doubting God. I thought I had worked through this. Apparently my heart struggled to believe what my head understood. Instead of trying to answer the question for me, my group responded with a greater gift:

encouraging me to ask God this question during the time of silence.

So I asked Him this simple, complicated, and loud question. Then I set it aside, not wanting to answer it myself with what I knew cognitively about God. Cognitive understanding obviously wasn't enough. I turned to Julian of Norwich, wanting God's revelations of divine love for her to take root in my heart too. Eventually I reached her vision of "a lord who has a servant". And here God responded to my doubt. In this vision a servant goes eagerly to do his master's bidding but disastrously falls into a pit:

> And immediately, [the servant] falls into a deep pit and receives very great injury. Then he groans and moans and wails and writhes, but he cannot rise up nor help himself in any way.
>
> In all this, the greatest misfortune that I saw in him was the lack of reassurance, for he could not turn his face to look back upon his loving lord (who was very near to him and in whom there is complete reassurance), but like a man who is feeble and witless for the moment, he was intent on his suffering and waited in woe. . . . I watched deliberately to see if I could discover any failure in him, or if the lord would

> allot him any blame, and truly there was none seen—for only his good will and his great desire were the cause of his falling, and he was as willing and as good inwardly as when he stood before his lord ready to do his will.
>
> And in the same way, his loving lord constantly watched him most tenderly.[58]

My head snapped back, returning to these words I had to reread: "I watched deliberately to see if I could discover any failure in him, or if the lord would allot him any blame, *and truly there was none seen*" (emphasis mine). My heart caught inside. In the lecture setting, I had not realized these words were for me. More than an answer, I heard God's reassurance.

Is this my fault, God?

Truly there is none, Juli. There is no shame in falling. And if you are clinging to fault, you cannot receive My reassurance, comfort, and help. You don't have to make this right. You can't. Let Me.

In time and with help, I came to realize this was more than an answer to one question. Julian, as an observer of this vision, helped me to assess the situation for fault. But I wasn't an observer. I was the servant, and I was still in the pit. This was a window into my present reality. So from the dark hole I continued to listen. God had more to say:

Juli, I am proud of you. I wouldn't change what you did because you were following Me with all your energy. I love you more than words can say. Can you stay with this present darkness if you know I am not disappointed in you, and I'm not somewhere else? I am for you and with you in this dark place.

With a deep, steadying breath, I answered. *Yes.*

God handed me a lens of love again. This time I experienced the love with which God sees *me*, even when (perhaps *especially* when) I fall.

When we see through love, we grasp what's most real about ourselves.

During that same week, I engaged in a fresh way with an experience Jesus had with an invalid (John 5). Jesus found this unnamed man by a crowded pool that was believed to provide healing. I imagined myself in this scene, observing their interaction from ground level. I watched Jesus approach the invalid, then witnessed the invalid's striving, comparisons, and excuses. The needy man's resistance frustrated me. Jesus, in contrast, was drawn to his pain and brokenness. He moved closer and engaged with compassion and mercy. I admired that. More so, I *desired* that. I wanted to see others with eyes of love as Jesus did. I wanted to move closer with my heart instead of keeping separate with my head. So I asked Him for this. It seemed like another place God wanted to offer me heart-shaped glasses, this time as a way to see others.

It brought to mind something I had read from Roberta Bondi recently:

> We moderns assume that love blinds because we believe that somehow we see people as they really are only when we see them at their worst. We know that secretly Mary is slovenly, or John is a crook, or Susan is only interested in herself. When we find people's flaws after a long acquaintance with them, we believe we are finally seeing the truth about them. Our Christian ancestors thought exactly the opposite: we see people as they really are only when we see them through the tender and compassionate eyes of God. It is this kind of vision that is essential to being truly rational.[59]

**When we see through love, we grasp
what's most real about others.**

Heart-shaped glasses changed everything—the way I see situations, myself, and others. But it wasn't as simple as Jesus leaving them on a bench, and then I see differently. It's been more like walking with Jesus through my days. Something happens. I get frustrated. He nudges me and whispers, *Put these on, and look again*. Often I've needed to pause, take a breath, then look beyond and below the surface. I'm learning to notice, then lay aside my impulsive reactions and ask God for His eyes, His heart, His way forward.

"Do you believe he is doing the best he can?" James's therapist once asked me.

The question unsettled me. *I want to. I should.*

"If your default is to never believe James, how will you know when or if he is being honest?"

Again, I didn't have an answer, just a strong gut feeling that what I currently saw on the surface wasn't honest or real.

But these questions also challenged me. Am I always believing the worst? God says that love "believes all things"(1 Corinthians 13:7 NRSV), but I didn't know what that meant anymore. Why couldn't I see any good? I had spent so much time digging, investigating, uncovering what lay below the surface-level, perfect performance because it seemed too good to be true. And frequently I was right: what I found underneath wasn't consistent.

I had become adept at unearthing the problem, but in the process lost sight of or hope for anything deeper than the problem. So I began to ask, "God, help me to see as You see." And slowly He began to exchange my thick prescription lenses for His heart-shaped glasses.

Shortly after these sight lessons, I had a real conversation with James—our first real conversation in almost a year. I listened and answered his questions honestly.

Without anger or judgment, I gave a sober assessment of what I saw and how I felt. I didn't hold back the troubling things I saw underneath the surface. There was room in the conversation and permission for him to correct me if he needed. Then I shared what I saw underneath the "underneath" things—deeper realities, desires, longings, and purpose. And something broke open in him. A memory from way below the surface flooded to the top. He shared it in an unguarded moment. And I was overwhelmed with the God who at this moment gave me His eyes. I witnessed the miraculous impact of seeing with His love.

It didn't make everything better all at once. But there is hope in learning to see with a love that helps me, and those around me, grasp what's most real.

And when we see through love, we discover that "There lives the dearest freshness deep down things."[60]

God's Grandeur
Gerard Manley Hopkins

The world is charged with the grandeur of
    God.
  It will flame out, like shining from shook foil;
It gathers to a greatness, like the ooze of oil
  Crushed. Why do men then now not reck his
    rod?
Generations have trod, have trod, have trod;
  And all is seared with trade; bleared, smeared
    with toil;

And wears man's smudge and shares man's
   smell: the soil
 Is bare now, nor can foot feel, being shod.

And for all this, nature is never spent;
  There lives the dearest freshness deep down
   things;
And though the last lights off the black West
   went
  Oh, morning, at the brown brink eastward,
   springs —
Because the Holy Ghost over the bent
  World broods with warm breast and with ah!
   bright wings.[61]

The sunglasses I found on a bench beside the Lake of St. Mary in November in Chicago. They help me see better than all my other glasses. My need for them is a constant.

Campfire Conversation
Glasses

1. How might fear or sadness be distorting your clarity? Have you given much thought to your blind spots? Are you open to receiving counsel from trusted others? How are you integrating this counsel into your present life?

2. Have you ever asked God to help you see how He has been with you in a previous season (His posture, demeanor, intentions, working)? Were you surprised by what surfaced from that request? What did it reveal to you about the nature and character of God? Did it change your understanding of Him? Or did it alter your relationship with Him in any way? If you've not done this, are you open to asking God this kind of question? Why or why not?

3. Where do you need God's Spirit to hover over brokenness? Where do you need God to help you frame a situation or person (maybe yourself, maybe all the above) in love? To move from judgment to compassion? Have you/can you ask Him for this?

4. Does Julian's vision of "a lord who has a servant" sync or resonate with how you know and experience God? Or yourself? How so or not?

15

The Arena

*G*rowing up, I probably attended more sporting events than most, both in quantity and in variety. My dad was the athletic director at our large local high school, so ensuring these events ran smoothly was his responsibility. Many late afternoons we might catch him at a swim meet, baseball game, or tennis match. On Saturdays it was wrestling or volleyball tournaments.

But Friday night basketball games are what I remember best. This was Indiana high school basketball at its finest: season tickets, pre-game light shows, intense rivalries, and a packed arena that drew most of our community to its bleachers. All this was great, but for me the real magic happened after the crowds left. My dad would work after the games, giving me, my siblings, and friend a few tasks, and then we were free. Hide-and-seek was a favorite. We also practiced Olympic gymnastics routines on the equipment behind the upstairs bleachers. And we scoured the stands for used paper Pepsi cups that became Wonder Woman armbands in our weekly fight against crime.

Our basketball team was good, so the games were exciting, but it was so much more for me. As I grew older, I became an active participant as an athlete myself. And then my boys became the participants. That's when sports slowly lost their magic for me. I think I got too caught up in the results of the games, assuming my boys needed success to be okay, losing sight of the gifts of connection, contributing to a team, growing through perseverance, and playing for fun and the love of the game.

I've witnessed similarities between my experience with sports and my engagement with prayer. In both sports and prayer, I eventually focused mostly on results. This path was marked by stressing out and trying harder, piling up and on, all while experiencing a slow leak of energy and hope. What I failed to recognize was that all along, the challenges and struggles in both spaces are where I've learned and grown. That's also where I discovered greater gifts like the heart of God, a deeper connection with my boys, and a real sense that all will *truly* be well.

Though I knew better from my childhood, I started living as if sports were only about winning and success. And I fell for the lie that my boys needed that to be okay.

Likewise, for many years I thought prayer was simply asking God for what I wanted and needed to be well. That often looked like various versions of "Please help _____ to be [some version of] happy and successful." And if I didn't get that, then I concluded that I must not have asked the right way. Or worse, I concluded that God wasn't listening and didn't care.

Years later, I read Dallas Willard, who described prayer as "talking to God about what we are doing together."[62] I agree . . . even when what we are doing together is walking at the park, reading a book, or sitting by a fire. Maybe more in those places than anywhere else, prayer loses its results focus and becomes beautifully relational. Through intimate relationship, good things tend to come. And they often come slowly and with some struggle. Our adoption story precipitated an unexpected prayer journey, one in which I eventually discovered greater gifts.

On James's twelfth birthday I began a prayer journal for him. Whenever I came across a scripture in the Bible, a line in a song, a phrase from a book, or a concept someone shared that brought James to mind—that filled a gap or articulated a need—I personalized it, fitting its details to our details. These were big requests for healing, wholeness, and peace in our home and hearts. I was desperate for this. Life as it currently functioned was not sustainable. We needed help.

It took a few years to fill the journal cover to cover. During this time I engaged with hope and energy. I sensed God's leading to pray boldly, and I trust He heard. But I didn't see any answers. Over time the magic faded; hope exhaled. And once the journal filled, I didn't grab another. I paused. I didn't stop praying for James, but I no longer had a practice dedicated to this effort.

During this season of prayer, I laid my big requests before God. It was as if Jesus were asking me, as He asked many others, "What do you want Me to do for you?" And I laid it out. These desires I shared with God never die. They live on in His heart. He remembers. I'm the one who wants immediate results. I tend to hurry healing, or at least I try. God, in contrast, goes slowly. He starts small and usually inside of me.

Sometime later I heard Richard Foster speak of carrying prayers for what seemed a very long time. After eleven months of daily praying the same short prayer, he said he was just beginning to sense some things shift within himself. His posture was intentional and persevering. His focus was simple and internal (self, but not *selfish*). This was a different conversation with God. As Foster shared his prayer, I knew what mine was. Tucked within the writings of George Buttrick, a simple prayer waited for me, one that fit: "Bless So-and-so whom I foolishly regard as an enemy. Bless So-and-so whom I have wronged. Keep them in Thy favor. Banish my bitterness."[63]

I needed that prayer in a way that's hard to describe. It felt like taking a vitamin for a particular deficiency, and it actually made me feel better over time. I filled in the blanks and carried this prayer, whispering it daily, sometimes continuously. Over time my heart softened and strengthened. This prayer sustained me during face-to-face encounters. I found a greater capacity to show up and be present in hostile environments.

This prayer paved the way for a conversation with James that I would describe as a miraculous breakthrough. James approached me about a decision we had made that he disagreed with. I showed up to our conversation less fearful and reactive. And the Holy Spirit brought a memory to mind for James of God's faithfulness and goodness, and my and my husband's role in that. James expressed genuine remorse about his posture of long-held distrust, as well as awe, gratitude, and a desire to trust God going forward. He shared his desire to change, to go a different direction. And for one of the first times, this felt honest.

And then . . . nothing. Just as quickly as that door within James opened, it shut, locked tight—he even added reinforcements. Flooded with disappointment and hurt, I lacked energy to pray at all. I went through the motions, but the Buttrick prayer felt dry and heavy. Honestly, the only prayer I connected with was from an article I read: "God, would you clean up all the [crap] in [James's] head?"[64] William Vaswig, a well-loved and respected pastor and minister of healing prayer, had once prayed these surprising words over a young man. I figured if it worked for him, it might work for me too. And though I was desperate, and this felt honest, God didn't bring much life from it. I suppose the heart of a prayer matters to God more than the words we use. And my heart was tired.

A small group of friends covered this gap when I shared it. In my weariness, they responded with energized and hopeful prayer, giving thanks for the breakthrough, for the "crack" of openness in James, as they called it several times. With that word my mind returned to a recently hiked trail dotted with hazelnuts. Many of them had split open at the end, where a tiny green sprout extended and burrowed into the hard ground. The start of new life . . . and it only required a crack. The nut wasn't split wide open. The shell wasn't smashed. The smallest of cracks allowed life to emerge. I was holding out for an apology and a right-setting of broken relationships. And God was encouraging me, *It takes only a tiny crack. And a crack is what you have. Receive with thanks. I've given you enough. Give it space and let it grow.* Hurry had begun to show up in me again, and God responded with a community of support, a hopeful picture of work in process, and a way to persevere.

Many months later I found myself in a prayer circle of new friends. And someone introduced a new way to pray, a wordless prayer. He guided us through a visualization, imagining a spark of light beginning in our chest, expanding outward. As it grew, it illuminated the body, bringing warmth, peace, and a sense of well-being. The spreading light scattered darkness—like fear, anger, anxiety, and hopelessness.

I imagined this light as the Holy Spirit: first in myself,

and then in others. A warmth and well-being settled in me. I began to pray for James in this new way. In my mind's eye, light emerged from a crack within James. As it spread, I saw him gradually fill with light, warmth, peace, and real joy. Even his face was softer, more transparent.

Words were not required. And I had expended many words over the years. They had long since rung hollow. I embraced this way to be with God, without words. One morning as I prayed, Jesus entered the picture. I watched in wonder as He came and placed his hands on James's chest, bringing the light through His touch. Another day I sensed Jesus asking me to join Him. I was fearful, but He accepted my hesitancy. I continued to watch in prayer. He continued to invite me. Soon I found myself placing my hand on top of His hand, on James's heart— such a strange and beautiful way to pray. In all my years of learning and practicing prayer, no one ever taught me this. All the same, it felt real and right. Nothing was forced or strained, which made the strange feel natural. It was like these song lyrics coming to life: *"Lord, teach me to pray. Not just words, not what to say. But my heart, where it should lay. O Lord, teach me to pray."*[65] The Lord taught me to pray without words through an actual embodied experience.

And then I heard some news about James that abruptly deflated me, and like a popped balloon, I fizzled out. Again my hope disappeared. Again my energy drained. All efforts felt in vain.

I shared my disappointment with God. And He

soon provided a message that held something solid to stand on where the ground under me had crumbled: "Human life that is animated and lived through the Spirit generates some kind of exponential and death-defying good. Not just good. It's categorically different" (Ashley Matthews).[66]

I had experienced the Holy Spirit animating my prayers, bringing them to life and taking them over. *I didn't anticipate Jesus showing up in that visualized prayer. I didn't plan to place my hand with His over James's heart and see light break through.* That was categorically different. And God was encouraging me that this was *good*. He was asking me to trust Him, regardless of the way things appeared. There was exponential and death-defying good happening within James, no matter the mess on the surface.

I felt a measure of peace, and I continued to pray this way for a while. But honestly, my energy wasn't there. Eventually I stopped altogether and felt bad, as if I weren't doing my job. Then one day, through the words of a song that I can't even remember now, I sensed God whisper, *I'm still praying this way for James. I come every day with Light and Life for him. You can rejoin me when you're ready. But there's no rush, just an invitation. I am taking care of this. And I am bringing the light to you too.*

The gentleness and undeserved gift of this blew me away. God is not, surely not, a Father to whom I merely hand my broken things for Him to fix. He is not set on a short-term plan of making all things (like me and my boys) happy and successful. He doesn't put that expectation on us. And thank goodness! Gosh, the pressure … to perform, to succeed, to win, and be happy all the time would just be too much. It'd be such a surface-y, shallow, high-pressure existence. That's where the magic goes to die, along with relationship, connection, and all good things.

Instead, I've come to know God more like a Father who invites me to show up in the arena where He's working and join Him as I can. He likes it when I'm there, and He enjoys how I enjoy being there. He is in charge. I am a recipient of and participant in His deep goodness and love. This is more than happy and successful. This, I think, is contentment—at peace in a full and satisfied way, regardless of whether I win or lose today.

I don't need to win the game or be the star. Some days are for resting and playing, learning to wait for and with my Father. In other words, sometimes being Wonder Woman is more than enough.

Jeffersonville High School, William S. Johnson Arena, 1988. Lots of energy. Lots of people cheering, laughing, and sweating. I was there and have no idea who scored the most points or won that game. But being present, participating in my own way, shaped me for the good. May I bring this energy, this desire to enjoy and partici-pate in something bigger than me, into the arena with God.

My dad took his job seriously. He was good at what he did. He also liked to have fun and play jokes on his friends. On this occasion, though, the joke was on him. Several of his friends who had been recipients of his "fun" turned the tables this Friday night, and moments before tip-off, the announcer called him to the scorer's bench, where a belly dancer performed for his birthday.

God wants to laugh with us. God wants to surprise us. God wants us to relax and enjoy Him, even as we work hard and persevere through struggle. Not every moment with Him needs to be intense and serious. Life with God is so much bigger than that.

Laughter Came from Every Brick

Teresa of Ávila

Just these two words He spoke
changed my life.
"Enjoy me."
What a burden I thought I was to carry—
a crucifix, as did He.
Love once said to me, "I know a song,
would you like to hear it?"
And laughter came from every brick in the street
and from every pore in the sky.
After a night of prayer,
He changed my life when He sang,
"Enjoy me."[67]

Campfire Conversation
The Arena

1. Has anything in life lost its magic for you? What might have caused that? Have you/can you ask God for insight? Do you feel pressure to be more engaged—or feel the freedom to be where you are? Do you have a sense of God there? What is that like?

2. Where do you feel responsible for results? Where is God in that? What might He want you to see, know, or do in that situation or relationship?

3. What do you want most for your loved ones? Have you/can you share this with God? How might wanting success and happiness for someone increase the pressure on him or her instead of helping him or her? What might God want most for your loved ones?

4. How do you pray? (meaning, how do you engage relationally with God?) Does this feel connecting to you? Do you have a sense of God being present with you? Responding to you? Is there energy there? Could God be inviting you into new spaces and ways of connecting with Him? What reservations do you have? Maybe you could begin to shift a little, if you want to, by asking God what a new way of being with Him might look like.

5. Do you enjoy God? Do you want to? Have you shared this with Him recently?

_____

_____

_____

_____

_____

_____

_____

_____

_____

_____

_____

_____

_____

_____

_____

_____

_____

_____

Bugs

With practiced casualness, my friend reached over and said, "Hold still."

That was all it took. I froze, sucked in my breath, and squeaked, "Get it off!"

I knew it was a bug, and I just don't like them. Over the past eight years and hundreds of miles walked together, I had shared all my bug stories with her . . . the roach, the tick, the lice. She knew them all, and she knew me. Small things can undo me.

Well, the roach wasn't so small. It was quite large actually.

So it was no surprise that near the end of an interesting, albeit long day of spiritual formation lectures, my head snapped at the mention of bugs—the eggs of bugs, to be more precise. *Logismoi* are the small, frequent—and often obscure and unnoticed—thoughts that equip us for bad works. But the word picture associated with them, I learned, is *maggot eggs*. Yuck. Our lecturer Chris Hall shared that *logismoi* (assaultive thoughts and false reasonings in the context of his lecture) lay suggestions like eggs in our minds.[68] Thoughts grow into mindsets that grow into corrupt words and actions. The nasty little eggs hatch a nasty larger atmosphere.

And they quench the big goal: to love. Finding these bad boys when they are small and in the dark isn't easy, but it's important. *Logismoi* include such things as "worries, temptations, doubts, self-accusations, cynical thoughts, mental 'stewing,' rehearsal of past injuries, scheming, imagined conversations, and distracting or obsessive thoughts."[69] Hall named examples such as "You'll never change," "Just a little won't hurt," and all sorts of other "what ifs" and "if onlys."

I wondered which *logismoi* I'm most susceptible to. Pretty quickly a few came to mind: "This is your fault," "You should have done more," "You need to do something now!" "What's the point?" "How selfish!" While always susceptible to such voices, our difficult season with James had turned up the volume, the frequency, and my sensitivity. Sometimes these voices came from the outside. Others were strictly in my head.

A couple of years into our adoption journey, we reached a place of needing more support than our home could provide. With professional help, we made a difficult, humble, and hopeful transition to residential therapy for James. This provided me with unexpected space to focus on *my* healing.

One of the first steps I took was attending a five-day spiritual formation retreat where Roberta Bondi introduced me to early Christianity, through the desert fathers and mothers (third-century Christians who lived in solitude in the Egyptian deserts). They in turn introduced me to the "passions": habitual ways of seeing and perceiving that distort and inhibit love.[70] Passions derive from *logismoi*.

The root word of *passion* in Latin means "to suffer," which is perhaps why Anthony the Great, a desert father from AD 300, called these the great wounds that affect all humankind. Their effect is to take away our freedom to love, and real freedom is always a freedom to love (not a freedom to be as bad as we want).[71]

Passions include things like anger (irritable, reactionary, or resentful attitudes as a constant state of mind), gluttony (expending a lot of energy on food), avarice (being unwilling to share, stemming from fear of future), impurity (lust), acedia (restless boredom), vainglory (needing to be liked), and pride (devaluing others compared to self).[72] Roberta Bondi wisely explained that the healing of the passions comes through self-awareness and small steps, not by placing blame and trying harder. And she said we can expect this healing to take a long time.[73] Peace and wholeness don't come from understanding and figuring it all out. They come by actively trusting the One who does.

This laid a strong foundation for the healing work God was about to do within me. I had no idea that helping James move to a healing place would create room for my own healing.

Years later I returned to the passions and found tucked within *Glittering Vices*, by Rebecca Konyndyk DeYoung, something that jumped off the page. *Pusillanimity* is a vice (or passion) that means smallness of soul. According to DeYoung, Thomas Aquinas described the pusillanimous as those who "shrink back from what God has called them to be." The pusillanimous "rely on their own puny powers and focus on their own potential for failure, rather than counting on God's grace to equip them for great work in his kingdom."[74] DeYoung pointed out that "seeing ourselves is difficult. Sometimes we need to hear a precise diagnosis from someone else, and to hear it at a particular time."[75]

Well, here I had my diagnosis. Pusillanimity showed up in me as constant self-doubt, wavering, second-guessing, staying too quiet, long hesitations, non-responsiveness, and lack of follow-through. Being seen was motivating as well as precise. The diagnosis came with an urging; there was more beyond it: life, purpose, and freedom.

Somewhere along the way I had lost my voice— the very voice God had given me. My voice was meant to extend love, but it had gotten really, really quiet. And even when speaking up wasn't appropriate or helpful, pusillanimity distracted and depleted me from engaging in the life right in front of me. Loving efforts drained out of me from a fear of doing or saying the wrong thing. With God's gentle direction, I began to see my timidity show up all over the place. This was a passion I had struggled with for a long time. I didn't suddenly "catch it" during our adoption journey. But our adoption crisis intensified my smallness of soul. So when pusillanimity showed up on the page in front of me, I recognized it. And having lived under it so long, I was ready for a larger life.

As new opportunities crossed my path to live bigger, take risks, speak up, and love, I saw them for what they were: soul-stretching practice with God. This was how I began to grow, to live toward *magnanimity*, a virtue meaning greatness of soul, a willingness to face danger and take action for noble purposes. Practicing magnanimity entailed risking awkward—clumsy, imperfect stepping out. The point was not the outcome, to make a name for myself, or to do big things in the eyes of the world. The point was the stretch itself, out of my comfort zone, taken with God because I chose to trust Him, not myself. Stepping out awkwardly and letting go of outcomes: that was the goal. Living larger was not dependent upon everything working out perfectly. Adoption certainly hadn't been a walk of perfection, but I found God present, loving, and shaping me, even so. Sharing my stories contained in this book was also a series of successive exercises in magnanimity.

Along the way God supplied oxygen for the invitations to step out. It wasn't just me gutting it out by willpower. That wouldn't last long or go far. David Benner wisely instructed that "love-shaped willing has a softness that teeth-gritting determination and discipline can never mimic. Love opens us up and makes us more alive, whereas determination makes us more closed and less vital."[76] I couldn't sustain this path toward magnanimity by discipline and determination alone. I couldn't simply pep-talk myself into a larger life.

However, when I showed up daily with willingness, something more organic and surprising happened. From a posture of openness, I discovered a spiritual practice that gradually pushed out small-souled voices, replacing them with audacious truth that I needed God's help to believe. In his book *Discovering Our Spiritual Identity*, Trevor Hudson shares a holy experiment of crafting a "beloved charter."[77] This statement, personally designed with God, reminds me of who I am to Him. These are soul-stretching words of love and purpose for myself that ultimately impact how available I am to others. It took me a long time to ask God for this and even longer to sit still and listen for His response. But I grew to deeply enjoy the late afternoon ritual of dropping whatever I was doing to sit in the sun with a cup of tea and picture Jesus saying this to me:

Juli, my every-day beloved, I want you to experience this as an anchor in a world that sways with praise and blame, acceptance and rejection, success and failure.

You don't need to compete. You don't need to try so hard to please others. In fact, the competing and trying distance you from Me.

Be yourself because your self delights Me. Be ordinary. Be small. Be different. Be spirited. Trust your inborn abilities as a safe place and a gentle voice. Zigzag among spaces that nourish. Hover and stay awhile. Rest whenever you need. Live outside the cages. Rebel. Persist. Walk away from that door. Show up as dust, knowing galaxies spiral inside you.[78]

I bless the largeness in you.[79] *I call it forth to shine, live free and unfettered, careless in My care, chasing My beauty, and letting it nourish.*

Over your past, I declare: you have done what you could. It was a beautiful offering. I accept gladly, without any hesitation. My heart is touched by how you've given yourself and are learning to love. I forgive and cover all your shortcomings. Leave the grave of failure and the tomb of timidity behind. Let's walk hand-in-Hand into what's next.

I am making you into your true self. Do not yield to fear. Yield to the largeness in you. I'm in that. Let it open. There is extraordinary magic—a crown of pearls within. I am achieving more than you long for, ask for, dream of. I am always right here—ever with you, working this out deeply and gently, within and beyond. And with our every step, you've got Me singing for joy.[80]

I shared about the discovery of pusillanimity and this beloved charter with my bug-swatting friend. She also shared the voices in her head, the mindsets they created, and her own desire to live free and love. We often paused after our walks to offer it all to God, coming to a posture of willingness at the end, asking for help and wisdom, and a way forward. At some point I realized I may always struggle with smallness of soul. There is no instant "cure."

But I know God holds a larger life for me. And He provides walking friends and holy experiments and so many other creative means to help me step into invitations that feel too much for me. When I choose to listen to His voice of love through safe friends, beloved charters, Scripture, music, nature, and even silence, then the nasty little voices have no place to lay maggot eggs in my mind. And the space within slowly becomes a place of beauty, goodness, and love . . . day by day by day. The larger I grow with God, the less the small things undo me and the more room I have for love. By this, He means to knock the bugs off my shoulders too. It turns out, He's also a good Friend who is not a fan of them either.

During that first spiritual formation retreat I attended, I spent a good amount of time reflecting near a pond that held this big, beautiful swan.

Years later, while learning to live larger, I was deeply encouraged by a poem by Rainer Maria Rilke. It depicted my small living as lumbering and awkward, like a swan walking on hard ground. (And here I thought staying small and in the background was keeping me safe and affording me the appearance of "normal," whatever that is.) In the poem the swan steps down into the water, nervously letting go of the ground that's supporting it. And by letting go, the swan discovers a more natural and beautiful habitat—a place it is meant for. It's just that scary letting-down into the water—that soul-stretching reach. And for that, there is God's ever-present help, receiving me with gladness, something like the water that receives and holds the swan, allowing it grace of movement and freedom in being. To me, this is a picture of learning to live magnanimously.

The Swan
Ranier Maria Rilke

This clumsy living that moves lumbering
as if in ropes through what is not done,
reminds us of the awkward way the swan walks.

And to die, which is the letting go
of the ground we stand on and cling to every day,
is like the swan, when he nervously lets himself down
into the water, which receives him gaily
and which flows joyfully under
and after him, wave after wave,
while the swan, unmoving and marvelously calm,
is pleased to be carried, each moment
more fully grown,
more like a king, further and further on.[81]

Campfire Conversation
Bugs

1. Where do small things tend to trip you up? What are your sensitivities? What might be the voices at work in these places—the *logismoi* such as worries, temptations, doubts, self-accusations, cynical thoughts, mental "stewing," rehearsal of past injuries, scheming, imagined conversations, and distracting or obsessive thoughts? What exactly are they saying in your head? (Naming these voices can help create greater awareness.)

2. Consider the passions (identified by the desert fathers as great wounds that affect all humankind and take away our freedom to love). Which ones seem to afflict you, hindering your ability to love?

   - Envy (measuring self-worth comparatively)[82]
   - Vainglory (an excessive and disordered desire for recognition and approval)[83]
   - Sloth (resisting and resenting the demands of love and the divine good within)[84]
   - Avarice (excessive love and desire for money and possessions)[85]
   - Wrath (desire for revenge and the injury of someone else)[86]

- Gluttony (focusing on the pleasure or particularities of food eaten to compensate for a lack of rest, joy, or peace)[87]
- Lust (excessive physical desires that reduce connection to fleeting pleasure)[88]
- Pride (devaluing or deemphasizing others compared to self)[89]

3. Each passion tends to have a virtue to offer in its place. What virtue might God desire to grow in you? Have you/can you ask Him? What would it look like to engage with God in practicing this virtue?

4. Spend some time with God crafting your own beloved charter. Trevor Hudson suggests incorporating phrases from Scripture. You can also look for quotes or lyrics from other learning spaces that resonate with you. Maybe look for things that intersect the virtues you and God desire to grow in you. This can be as short as four to five sentences. Set aside a few minutes each day, allowing God to speak these life-giving words over you. Let it adapt and change over time.

5. How might your self-protective ways actually be "lumbering and awkward"? What would it look like to trust God here?

You Win

James and I were once teammates in a gingerbread house-making competition. Our rivals were tough: a rocket scientist and accountant, a grandma/grandson duo, and two others with a magic touch who'd been known to slap things together and call it a day (with impressive results). My family is pretty competitive, and I can be too. I like to win—though it's no secret that in high school I might have thrown the third set when my tennis match went too long. "You win," I'd concede under my breath and shrug it off.

Typically, though, concession wasn't so easy. "You win!" is complicated. Acknowledging defeat carries strong and mixed emotions. The flip side of "You win" seems to be "I lose." With that comes the sting of defeat, a fear of missing out, the shame of falling short. Beyond that, doubts and questions arise, questions that could keep me up at night, such as "Am I good enough/is this good enough?"

But I've glimpsed another side of "You win," one that is more like a welcome surrender than a crushing defeat. One that is about discovering I am enough; therefore, I can let go and trust. I can stop fighting. And when I do, I find peace and freedom and life right where I am. There is enough (time, information, resources) for today; and I am enough right here.

I trace my learning back to a summer family camp when our boys were young. A wise teacher spoke of raising children in today's fast-paced, high-pressure, very visible world. She recalled her own struggle with keeping up, measuring up, and producing children who were successful, kind, happy, and well-respected. She fought this until one day, at the end of her rope and resources, she opened her front door and shouted, "You win!" To her neighbors and friends, school and church community, and culture at large she declared, "Your child is smarter. Your child is a better athlete. Your daughter is more popular. Your son is going to a better college. Yours scored more goals. Yours is more thoughtful. Yours is funnier . . . volunteers more . . . goes to church more . . . has a better job. You are a more loving parent. You. Win."

And with that, she chose to exit the competition. She stood against a culture, world, and community of scarcity, judging from the outside, keeping up, and never enough. She stopped fighting, pushing, and promoting (and oh, how subtly and pervasively we find ways to promote ourselves and our children). This was her "enough!"

After that, she became more aware of when she was slipping back into that mindset, when the temptation of doing enough and trying harder inched closer. And when it did, whether during a bus stop conversation about how busy everyone's children were, or a friend's Facebook post of his or her child who was the leading scorer (again), or a prayer request at church for a tired son's missionary efforts, she would quietly whisper to herself, "You win."

I eagerly adopted this practice, engaging it imperfectly yet tasting its freedom. And then one beautiful evening a feast of freedom was spread before me. I showed up at church, feeling crunched by questions of adequacy and fears of the future. It was an evening of music, of simply listening to songs chosen to help us connect with God, to supply words where we were out of words. I brought my discouragement and weariness, letting these songs of God's faithfulness simply wash over me. The last song of the night was upbeat—pure praise, offering our admiration and gratitude with joy-filled hallelujahs.

I watched the people around me, worshiping and celebrating Jesus. And it occurred to me: this was our collective "You win." You win, Jesus. You are perfect. You are enough. I can't compete. I can't measure up. I can't do what You do. I can't love the way You love. I can't heal anyone or save anyone. But *glory*, *hallelujah*, You can!

And this isn't about me trying harder and doing more and measuring myself against Your perfection. This isn't about how I have messed up or fallen short or failed, *because it isn't about me*. It's about You. You are my enough. You are *our* enough. And this is where we can stop competing with one another, stop judging one another, stop judging ourselves, and simply celebrate together that You win. You *won*, in fact.

This is where I can stop reading scripture like a list of instructions I'm trying to keep up with or a checklist of dos and don'ts I'm striving to perform. Instead, I can see it as a description of the kingdom of heaven. Jesus, by His perfection, opened the doors to this kingdom and invited me in, as my imperfect self. When I step through those doors, I'm free to practice, with Him, *His* ways of loving and giving. In His kingdom there is enough of His kind energy to do my imperfect best and trust Him for what I lack. This is not an excuse to not put forth effort, but it is an acknowledgment I will fall short. And it's safe to admit it and ask for help. That, in fact, is the nature of His kingdom; that's the way it operates. And so I must choose: Do I want to live that way—vulnerable and dependent, like a child? Or do I want to keep fighting and competing for the applause and approval of others?

This picture of celebration reminded me of a song from Scripture:

> *Here he comes!* The Commander! The Mighty Lord of Angel Armies is on our side! The God of Jacob fights for us! . . . He's the one who makes conflicts end throughout the earth, breaking and burning every weapon of war. Surrender your anxiety. Be still and realize that I am God. (Psalm 46:7a, 9–10a TPT)

In that room full of worshipers and in my family who is broken with conflict, God is on *our* side. He fights for *us*. There is only one side. And it's His. It's not that He fights for us versus them. He fights for us, period. He fights for unity, for relationship, for adoption, for reconciliation. My human inclinations lead to divisiveness, angst, anger, hurt, and separation. But He is fighting for us. If I choose a side, if I elevate my position, then I'm fighting against Him. I even realized that I could actually play both sides in my own head: fighting for myself with defensiveness, validation, and slander, and fighting against myself with self-doubt while playing the devil's advocate. Both positions are about me. I'm full of me. And God provides the way out: surrender to the Commander. Fall in line with Him. Let Him lead. Surrender my anxiety. Trust silently. Cease all striving. Be still and wait for Him. He is the one who makes conflict end. And He will. I know that.

My church played another song that night, one that felt like a promise from God delivered right to my heart.

It was a song about the celebration to come after this earthly life.[90] A celebration with feasting and restoration. A celebration without weeping or opposing sides. As I sang, I could picture my family seated together around a table in collective agreement: He has done great things. He healed us. He restored us. He united us. He saved our lives . . . all our lives, together. That filled my heart in a needed place. It held a gentle assurance: *this ends well*.

St. John Chrysostom, an early Christian thinker, said a thief will not disturb a house where there is a party going on inside. That night I saw a party going on all around me as people sang "glory, hallelujah." And Jesus invited me into this ongoing, daily community celebration of Him. When this is my mindset, I discover there is enough . . . more than enough for all of us. In contrast, scarcity thinking prodded me from the outside and inside with threatening questions like "Are you just trying to get rid of me?" and "Is this my fault?" and "Am I doing enough?" But when I join the party, these questions shift to things like "Jesus, what does it look like to trust You here?" and "Jesus, what does loving this person look like today?"

When I remember to shift, I find what I need. I see a way forward. I learn more and more how to love. And I never do it alone. God invites me into celebrations all along the way if I'm looking for them.

James and I won the competition that day. The smart team overthought it. The duo over-ate tubes of icing. The "slap it together" strategy didn't pan out.

For a moment, James and I celebrated a small victory, but it passed too quickly. I can't say we are on the same team right now. And that seems like such a weird place to end this book. But this is what I know: "You win!" is also *We win.* And that Promised Day is coming. I cannot yet see it, but I feel it, and I know it. Glory, hallelujah!

A victory pose with our award-winning, masterpiece gingerbread house.

A celebration of color for the day that's been, with a hint of a promising and Promised Day that is coming. Painted by my friend Andrea of a favorite and familiar sunset spot on Lake Lanier in Georgia. While each sunset is unique, I've noticed a pattern in how the color changes from purple to navy to black. And then the first stars begin to appear. Slowly and silently. One by one.

My mom and I particularly love what we call "sparkly water time," when the sun is setting over water, and light dances on the surface. I've grown to appreciate and wait for "sparkly night time." Instead of wanting to fast-forward to the next sunrise, I am beginning to realize I have stories to tell of the dark. When the day winds down and things get noisy inside, I'm learning to go out and seek God. Sometimes Patience comes to sit on my lap, imploring me to stay. Sometimes Joy quietly takes my hand, assuring me all will be well. More often now, I can stay with God for the brilliant night.

Campfire Conversation
You Win

1. Where have you experienced the sting of defeat? The fear of missing out? The shame of falling short? What does that feel like? Do you have a sense of how God might have been present in those places? Have you ever asked Him for a sense of this?

2. Are you trying to win right now? An argument or point of view, a position (for yourself, your child, or other), recognition or approval, or something else? Do you ever notice a scarcity mentality (a focus on and thinking about limited supply/not enough) creeping into these spaces? Where is God in that? What might it look like to surrender the results without giving up? In which areas of your life do you need to say "enough" and exit the competition? What might that look like?

3. Is there an area in your life in which you need God to fight for unity? Have you asked Him for this? What might it look like for you to cooperate and participate with Him in this work?

4. Where/what/how might God be inviting you to celebrate with Him? What shape could that take presently?

Close of a Campfire

I have sat for hours and hours around a fire. Once it was for most of a gray, chilly day with a good book. But eventually it's time to move on—to go to sleep or work or do something else. As we leave this campfire, it would be good to reflect.

How have you felt warmed?
- sensed a new or greater awareness of God's presence and activity?
- or greater clarification around His invitations for you?

What has burned up?
- through letting go or turning around, what is no longer a focus or priority?

- how have you experienced a lightening of your load/responsibility?

And what hasn't?
- what remains for you?
- what remains with God?

What has the light illumined?
- how have you gained clarity about yourself?
- about God?
- about your circumstances?

What has lifted, like smoke, as a prayer to God?
- what desires and longings have you shared with Him?
- what needs have you named to Him?

How has this slow, unhurried space to reflect and be with God changed you?

How can you return for more conversation and connection with One who deeply enjoys your company?

This is why I wait upon you, expecting your break-through, for your Word brings me hope. I long for you more than any watchman would long for the morning light. I will watch and wait for you, O God, throughout the night. (Psalm 130:5–6 TPT) Painted by Andrea.

Notes

Prologue

1. https://www.radadvocates.org.

2. J. M. Lawler, C. E. Hostinar, S. Mliner, and M. R. Gunnar, *Development and Psychopathology* 26, "Disinhibited social engagement in post-institutionalized children: Differentiating normal from atypical behavior," 451–464.

3. https://www.radadvocates.org/post/reactive-attachment-disorder-the-rare-culprit-that-stifles-traumatized-kids-and-their-parents.

4. Nancy Newton Verrier, *The Primal Wound: Understanding the Adopted Child* (Murphys, CA. Gateway Press, 1993), 54.

5. Ibid.

6. https://ec1409ca-cfb8-44d4-9ded-17ed84478048.filesusr.com/ugd/c30adf_8d2a67db1a944a3591286da88e1d2ad0.pdf.

7. Verrier, *The Primal Wound*, 63.

8. M. Follan and M. McNamara, *Journal of Clinical Nursing* 23, "A fragile bond: adoptive parents' experiences of care for children with a diagnosis of reactive attachment disorder," no. 7–8, 1076, 1085.

9. Ibid.

10. Amor Towles, *A Gentleman in Moscow* (New York, Viking Press, 2016), 196.

Chapter One

11. Timothy Keller, *Galatians for You* (Epsom, UK: The Good Book Company, 2013), 154.

12. Dallas Willard and Timothy Keller offer fresh expressions of commonly used Christian language that I find helpful. You can find more information on some of these virtues

here: https://www.soulshepherding.org/dallas-willards-definitions/ and here, https://plentifulredeemer.wordpress.com/2013/05/19/tim-keller-on-the-fruit-of-the-spirit/.

Chapter Two

13. "Take My Hand", from the album *If It Takes Me Back to You*, by Lindsay McCaul, 2012.

14. Dallas Willard, *Renovation of the Heart* (Colorado Springs: NavPress, 2012), 132–133.

Chapter Four

15. The first two sentences are a slight tweaking of Hosea 14:4a (NRSV), and the last sentence is my summary of Hosea 14:5–6.

16. Again, this is a slight tweaking of Hosea 14:7a (NRSV), and then my summary of Hosea 14:7b.

17. Mark Batterson, *Draw the Circle: The 40 Day Prayer Challenge* (Grand Rapids: Zondervan, 2012), 52–53.

Chapter Five

18. Eugene Peterson, "On Spiritual Direction," Jan 6, 2006, https://imagodeicommunity.ca/on-spiritual-issues/on-spiritual-direction-by-eugene-peterson/.

19. https://www.blueletterbible.org/lexicon/h8150/esv/wlc/0-1/.

20. https://www.blueletterbible.org/lexicon/h25556/esv/wlc/0–1/.

21. Howard Thurman, *Jesus and the Disinherited* (Boston: Beacon Press Books, 1976), 19.

22. Ibid., 30.

23. Ibid., 35.

24. Ibid.

25. Ibid.

26. Ibid., 48.

27. Ibid., 58.

28. Ibid.

29. Ibid., 45.

30. Ibid., 99.

31. Gerald May, *Care of Mind/Care of Spirit* (New York: HarperCollins, 1992), 90–91.

32. William A. Barry S.J. and William J. Connolly, *The Practice of Spiritual Direction* (New York: HarperOne, 2009), 86–87.

Chapter Six

33. https://www.christynockels.com/happy-mothers-day/

Chapter Seven

34. http://kingsenglish.info/2011/03/26/the-apple-of-his-eye/.

35. http://www.biblestudytools.com/dictionary/apple-of-the-eye/.

36. http://kingsenglish.info/2011/03/26/the-apple-of-his-eye/.

37. James Finley, *Merton's Palace of Nowhere* (Notre Dame, IN: Ave Maria Press, 2003), 86.

Chapter Eight

38. Larry Warner, *Discernment, God's Will, and Living Jesus* (Oceanside, CA: Barefooted Publishing, 2016), 36.

39. Carol Hamblet Adams, *My Beautiful Broken Shell* (Eugene, OR: Harvest House Publishers, 1998).

40. Macrina Wiederkehr, *A Tree Full of Angels* (New York: HarperOne, May 2009), xiii.

41. G. B. Buttrick, *Prayer* (Nashville: Abingdon-Cokesbury Press, 1942), 36.

Chapter Nine

42. Macrina Wiederkehr, *A Tree Full of Angels*, (New York: HarperOne, May 2009), 10–11.

Chapter Ten

43. Dallas Willard, *The Divine Conspiracy* (New York: HarperCollins, 1997), 350.

44. Brené Brown, *Rising Strong* (New York: Spiegel & Grau, 2015), 114–115.

45. Henry Cloud and John Townsend, *Boundaries* (Grand Rapids: Zondervan, 1992), 95–97.

46. William P. Young, *Cross Roads* (New York: FaithWords, 2012), 205.

Chapter Eleven

47. "It Is Done" featuring David Walker, from the album *Trust You* by Grace Snellville Worship, 2017.

48. Thomas Keating, *The Human Condition* (Mahwah, NJ: Paulist Press, 1999), 39.

49. Ibid., 39–40.

50. Ibid., 38.

Chapter Twelve

51. Desmond Tutu and Mpho Tutu, *The Book of Forgiving* (New York: HarperOne, 2014), 9. Used with permission.

52. Coleman Barks, *A Year with Rumi* (New York: HarperOne, 2006), 313.

Chapter Thirteen

53. https://www.blueletterbible.org/lexicon/g3107/kjv/tr/0–1/.

54. Dallas Willard, *The Divine Conspiracy* (New York: Harper Collins, 1997), 100–103.

55. Dallas Willard, *The Kingdom of God Teaching Series*, May 2006, https://christianaudio.com/renovare-the-kingdom-of-god-teaching-series-willard-dallas-willard-audiobook-download.

56. Mariotto Albertinelli. Visitation. 1503. The Uffizi, Florence.

Chapter Fourteen

57. Gerard Manley Hopkins, *Bright Wings, Dappled Things: The Poems of Gerard Manley Hopkins SJ*, (Dublin, IrelandMessenger Publications, 2018), 35.

58. Fr. John-Julian, OJN, *The Complete Julian of Norwich* (Orleans, MA: Paraclete Press, 2009), 229.

59. Roberta Bondi, *To Love as God Loves* (Minneapolis: Fortress Press, 1987), 60, 61.

60. Hopkins, *Bright Wings, Dappled Things*, 35.

61. Ibid.

Chapter Fifteen

62. Dallas Willard, *The Divine Conspiracy* (New York: HarperCollins, 1997), 243.

63. *Devotional Classics*, edited by Richard J. Foster and James Bryan Smith (New York: HarperCollins, 2005), 90.

64. James Catford, *The Royal Touch, Healing and the Kingdom of God*, ConversationsJournal.com 10.2, Fall/Winter 2012, https://dallaswillardcenter.com/wp-content/uploads/2014/05/Catford-Royal-Touch.pdf.

65. "Teach Me to Pray" (live) [featuring Marty Reardon], by Trinity Music, on the album *As It Is in Heaven: A Live Worship & Prayer Album*, 2019. Used with permission.

66. Ashley Matthews, https://westside.atltrinity.org/updates/resurrection-part-2.

67. *Love Poems from God: Twelve Sacred Voices from the East and West*, translated by Daniel Ladinsky (New York: Penguin Group, 2002), 276. Used with permission.

Chapter Sixteen

68. Chris Hall, "Christian Spiritual Formation III: Invitations to Transformation in Prayer, Virtue, and Word," Renovaré Institute, Mundelein, IL, November 21, 2019.

69. John Uebersax, "Evagrius Ponticus and the 'Wanderer' Demon," https://catholicgnosis.wordpress.com/2008/11/11/evagrius-ponticus-and-the-wanderer-demon/.

70. Roberta Bondi, *To Love as God Loves* (Minneapolis: Fortress Press, 1987), 65.

71. Ibid., 66–67.

72. Ibid., 71–76.

73. Ibid., 78–79.

74. Rebecca Konyndyk DeYoung, *Glittering Vices* (Ada, MI: Brazos Press, 2009), 9.

75. Ibid., 10.

76. David Benner, *Desiring God's Will* (Westmont, IL: InterVarsity Press, 2015), 50.

77. Trevor Hudson, *Discovering Our Spiritual Identity* (Westmont, IL: InterVarsity Press Books, 2010), 29–30.

78. Jan Richardson, *Circle of Grace* (Orlando, FL: Wanton Gospeller Press, 2015), 90.

79. Sue Monk Kidd, *The Book of Longings* (New York: Viking Press, 2020), 22.

80. My personal "beloved charter," February 2021 based on Trevor Hudson's book *Discovering Our Spiritual Identity*, 29–30.

81. Robert Bly, *Selected Poems of Rainer Maria Rilke – Translation from the German and Commentary by Robert Bly* (New York: Harper Perennial, 1981), 141. Used with permission.

82. DeYoung, *Glittering Vices*, 44.

83. Ibid., 60.

84. Ibid., 79, 85–94.

85. Ibid., 99, 100.

86. Ibid., 117.

87. Ibid., 140, 145.

88. Ibid., 162, 165.

89. Bondi, *To Love as God Loves*, 76.

Chapter Seventeen

90. "We Will Feast in the House of Zion" from the album *Psalms* by Sandra McCracken, April 2015.

Acknowledgments

I dedicate this book to my boys. Words can be few in our home and so I wrote for you. Because you need to know this part of our story and dwell on these things, where there is life.

These stories have been influenced by safe and deep relationships. I'm grateful for my family, for spiritual friendships, spiritual directors, counselors, and Friday morning friends who've circled up with me as we share our stories along the way. I'm grateful to my mom, always nudging me to write. To Jeff, quietly supporting this dream. And to my friend, Andrea, for stepping out with me and sharing her gift of painting throughout this book (and elsewhere). You can find her here on Instagram: andreawarren2017

Electric Moon Publishing, LLC is a custom, independent publisher who assists indie authors, ministries, businesses, and organizations with their book publishing needs. Services include writing, editing, design, layout, print, e-book, marketing, and distribution. For more information please use the contact form found on www.emoonpublishing.com.